PURPOSE + PROFIT

George Serafeim

PURPOSE
+
PROFIT

HOW BUSINESS CAN
LIFT UP THE WORLD

HarperCollins
LEADERSHIP

An Imprint of HarperCollins

Published by HarperCollins Leadership, an imprint of HarperCollins
Focus LLC.

Any internet addresses, phone numbers, or company or product
information printed in this book are offered as a resource and are not
intended in any way to be or to imply an endorsement by HarperCollins
Leadership, nor does HarperCollins Leadership vouch for the existence,
content, or services of these sites, phone numbers, companies, or
products beyond the life of this book.

ISBN 978-1-4002-2642-9 (eBook)

ISBN 978-1-4002-3035-8 (HC)

Library of Congress Cataloging-in-Publication Data
Library of Congress Cataloging-in-Publication
application has been submitted.

Printed in Canada

22 23 24 25 26 LSC 10 9 8 7 6 5 4 3 2 1

CONTENTS

CONTENTS

INTRODUCTION

I have to begin with a confession. When I was starting my career, I would not have picked up this book. It's not that I didn't care about whether businesses were helping the world, or whether purpose and profit could coexist. I just didn't think such topics were relevant to my life. I began my career analyzing and valuing insurance companies. Whether or not they were helping the planet in a broader sense than making a profit for their shareholders, providing a good living for their employees, or serving their customers with the products they sold weren't the most prominent questions on my radar.

I went to business school expecting to expand on the work I had been doing. I loved the intellectual challenge of diving into the technical aspects of valuation and really understanding complex financial instruments. I emerged with a doctorate from Harvard Business School in the era of the great financial crisis. My research on deeply technical issues was gaining traction and being published in some of the most prestigious academic journals in my field. I was fortunate upon graduation to receive offers to join the faculty of several top universities.

Still, something was missing.

One day, I was talking with a good friend, Ioannis Ioannou, a strategy professor at London Business School. Ioannis and I had overlapped in the doctoral program at Harvard and had long wanted to work together, but we had not yet found the time or identified an overlap in our research interests. He asked if I knew anything about companies that were making efforts to improve their impact on society. We began talking about issues like businesses treating their workers better, reducing pollution, and acting with integrity. We wondered why these issues were seldom considered as important as shareholder profits, and whether there was actually any data to support the commonly held view that doing things with social good in mind distracted from the core mission of a business and inevitably became a drag on performance.

As we reflected on these questions, I realized we did not have great answers. These discussions led me to reconsider the work I had been doing, and if it was truly the most impactful use of my skills and knowledge. I cared about the papers I was writing, but I wasn't sure if they filled me with a sense of purpose. I wanted to do more, and quickly discovered that the more I dove into thinking about companies and their impact on society, the more these issues mattered to me.

The truth is that I did not know why some companies behaved with an eye toward a greater purpose, and why some chose not to. I didn't know what the consequences were or even how to begin to analyze them. I did know that the world was a very complex place, and trying to understand how companies behave was inherently complicated. I also knew that if Ioannis and I took on this challenge—to explain the actions of companies and whether there were lessons to learn from their behavior—we would be fighting an uphill battle when it came to the data. Very few companies back then released data on measures such as diversity in the workforce, accidents, benefits provided to employees, carbon emissions, water consumption, or the access and affordability of their products. This was a big problem. How could we evaluate and understand the role of business in society if we did not have data?

Armed with the data we did have, we first tried to understand whether investors cared about the efforts of companies acting with a larger purpose in mind. Analyzing data on thousands of companies, we were able to show that Wall Street analysts were in fact issuing more pessimistic investment recommendations for firms making efforts to improve their impact on society than for those that weren't. The investment community seemed to hold the staggering belief that having a positive social impact was a signal that a company would perform worse than its peers in the future. How could we be living in a world where managers were penalized for doing good? More important, were these forecasts right? And if they were, what made them so? If doing good really did hamper a company's future performance, should we accept that reality, or could we instead work to change it? How, for instance, could we create the conditions for a society in which doing good would lead to doing well?

Doing the work was tough. Convincing people to take the work seriously was even tougher. The paper based on that research took us five (!) years to publish in a top academic journal. I was shocked at how little the academic world was considering these issues, especially since my archival and field research was convincing me that these issues were becoming more important for many in the business world, from CEOs to investors to employees and even to consumers looking to better understand the companies with which they engage. Yet there was so much resistance, so much unwillingness to consider the idea that social and environmental issues could be relevant and meaningful for business.

Many people in business saw these issues as "soft" and outside the scope of what a serious person should be thinking about. In 2011, I presented a piece of my research to an audience of about one hundred senior investment professionals across major financial institutions. The feedback was unanimous: "These topics are irrelevant." Not one person followed up with me to express an interest in understanding the data or exploring the work further. As a faculty member hoping to earn tenure, I recognized this was becoming a very risky adventure, as publishing in this nascent field was so difficult. Several friends, having my best interests in mind, gave me some simple advice to secure my career and my academic future: "Drop it."

I didn't want to drop it. By that point, my analysis and study of the behavior of companies, investors, and policymakers had led me to form the hypothesis that climate change, diversity and inclusion, access and affordability to products and services, product safety and quality, and opportunity in the workplace were examples of issues not just important in society but critical in business. I knew that the way to make people understand this—and not simply dismiss the ideas as soft—had to involve continued (and continuous) generation and analysis of objective data.

I went on a mission to create the metrics and the quantitative infrastructure needed to deeply understand how companies were behaving, and give them the evidence they needed to change the way they impact society. The data my colleagues and I began to generate supported my instincts. Environmental and social issues were indeed starting to affect valuation, profitability, and capital efficiency across many companies, many sectors of the economy, and many countries. An emerging field was forming around these environmental, social, and governance (ESG) issues, and an incredible amount of energy was unleashed across entrepreneurs, professionals, and investors with whom I was collaborating around the world.

I grew convinced that I could and should continue playing an active role in creating the conditions in which businesses could contribute to the well-being of society and the environment. Instead of asking, "Are these efforts relevant?" I realized the better question was, "What needs to happen to make these issues as relevant as they can be?" Reframing the question changed my perspective and allowed me to use my positions as scholar, educator, and practitioner to move the world forward in a productive and meaningful way.

In the years since, my colleagues and I have helped lead a revolution in how people think about these issues. As can be seen in our published research findings over the past decade, we have found that purpose-driven organizations and companies improving their performance on material ESG issues outperform their competitors by more than 3 percent annually in terms of stock returns.[1] In just one specific example, companies that responded to the COVID-19 pandemic with concrete efforts to protect customers, employees, and suppliers outperformed their peers by 2 percent in the one month covering the stock market collapse in March 2020.[2] While that data is impressive, it's important to recognize that it is not only the data that has changed (and continues to change) people's thinking. The collision of purpose and profit has emerged from larger shifts in society as well.

In Part I of this book, "Alignment: Creating Opportunity for Greater Corporate Purpose," I discuss several trends that have coincided to bring together the aims of business and the goals of society in new ways. Namely:

- The purpose of business is changing over time to reflect our desire for companies to contribute to the world (chapter one);
- Attitudes are evolving as people expect more from their jobs and customers expect more from the companies with which they do business (chapter two);
- Technology, social media, and new data metrics all give us far more visibility into the actions of companies than we've ever had, enabling vastly increased accountability around corporate behavior (chapter three); and
- Businesses are acting in very different ways than ever before, stepping up to provide public goods and filling a social role to yield positive results (chapter four).

In Part II, "Execution: How to Implement Purpose-Driven Initiatives," I switch the focus to how companies, investors, and employees can use these societal trends to drive impactful change in their businesses, their investments, and their lives. I'll discuss:

- How, tactically, companies can put the new analytics of doing good into practice and design initiatives that have positive impact (chapter five);

- The six archetypes of value creation enabled by these new trends (chapter six);
- The role of investors, and how their recognition that doing good can pay off in the capital markets is critical to keeping companies on the right path (chapter seven); and
- How we can all look at our choices and our careers through the lens of these societal trends, and manage our behavior to drive as much impact in our lives and for our organizations as we possibly can (chapter eight).

In the end, you will have a rich understanding of this movement in society, and actionable tips to implement these ideas in your own life and business. Figure 1.1 illustrates the book's big idea and shows where all of the pieces fit.

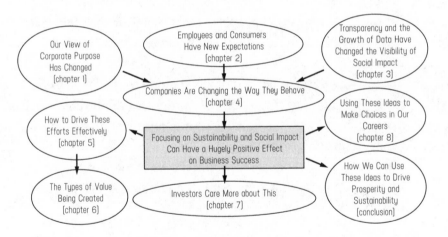

FIGURE 1.1

My work on these issues has played out in a way I never expected. All the trends you'll read about in Part I seemed to hit the public consciousness at once, and, seemingly overnight, interest in this field hit an inflection point. Suddenly, the ideas emerging from this research were reaching more receptive ears. I was getting more and more inquiries from business leaders and invitations to conferences. I started seeing real momentum and leaders taking action.

The data that I and others had been generating became too compelling to ignore, and society, for all of the reasons above, began to realize doing good and doing well didn't have to be mutually exclusive, at least not if you approached your sustainability strategies with care and intelligence. Organizations popped up like mushrooms, creating standards for ethical and sustainable investing and metrics to track performance, and governments have even started to require that social factors be considered when state and national retirement funds invest in companies. The Showtime drama *Billions*, which premiered in early 2016, made impact investing and sustainability key story lines in 2020—something that never would have been on the mainstream radar screen just a few years earlier.

When I started doing this work, more than one in eight S&P 500 companies did not have a single woman on their boards of directors. Barely a decade later, there isn't a single company without one (and women make up more than a quarter of all board seats—not ideal, of course, but it's progress).When I began, fewer than 20 percent of the world's biggest companies reported on the impact their businesses were having on the environment. Now, almost 90 percent have made it part of their annual reports.

In deep contrast to those early days, I now believe wholeheartedly that we live in a world where, quite fortunately, pursuing social goals and pursuing profit are becoming more and more aligned than ever before—for people at every level of an organization, at every age, and in every industry. The tension that many (including my students, as you'll see in chapter one) feel between the idea that people should go into business just to make money, and the realization that they themselves are motivated by more than that, is actually less complicated than they realize.

It still surprises me that not that many years ago, leaders would have doubted the mere notion that there could ever be a business benefit to acting with purpose and keeping sustainability, health, and the greater good in mind. There absolutely can be, though executing this successfully is not simple, and that's the real message of Part II. The biggest lesson I want to convey is that *merging purpose and profit is possible and can be tremendously rewarding, but it is not easy, and there are no guarantees.* Neither running a successful business nor contributing to meaningful social change is a simple undertaking. Both are tremendously challenging.

All I have to do to remember this is read my email. In the spring of 2021, I was getting set to teach my class about a local community development program that Southwire, an electrical wiring company in Carroll County, Georgia, had run successfully for years. As I was preparing for the class session, I received an email from a student explaining that he had been inspired by the success of this same program before he came to business school, when he was working with a Georgia chamber of commerce not far from Southwire's headquarters.

Southwire's success had been remarkable. In a school district where nearly a third of the students weren't graduating (almost half of the economically disadvantaged students in particular), Southwire collaborated with local school officials to find the most at-risk kids and put them on a path to finish high school. They took low-income kids with poor attendance, often with parents who were absent, abusive, addicted to drugs, or in prison, and gave them job training, mentorship, and a real opportunity to contribute. The program, known as 12 for Life, helped raise the graduation rate to 94 percent, even for the at-risk population. This made (and continues to make) a huge impact in the community and at the same time helps Southwire's business, bolstering employee morale by helping workers find meaning as mentors to students, allowing the company to attract and retain strong talent, and strengthening its social capital. The program has been profitable—and, as a result, sustainable—in both good and bad times, with any profits reinvested in scaling up the program and its impact. There are now thousands of proud 12 for Life alumni, as the program has expanded far beyond its initial vision.

My student had attempted to replicate the 12 for Life program in a different community, with a different type of company. "Spoiler alert," he wrote. "I failed." The details of why he failed are less important than the broader takeaway. These kinds of things fail all the time, and *execution is far more important than intention.* The student in this case cited several relevant factors: lack of enthusiasm from the company he was working with, lack of resources and commitment from the school system, and lack of strong leadership. It all added up to an unsatisfying result; the program never got off the ground.

I share this story to make it clear that this is not a book about the magic of doing good. The balance between business success and progress toward social and environmental reform, and the choices companies make about that balance, are always complicated, and the reactions of consumers, investors, and the broader world are not always predictable. Yes, my research shows that it pays off more and more, and in some cases is even becoming a requirement for survival. But in order to make it work on the ground, you need to dive deep and really understand why some programs succeed and some ultimately fail. That is what this book is about.

Figure 1.2 shows where *Purpose + Profit* falls along the spectrum of possible viewpoints. The left-hand side of the figure represents a traditional view of business: positive impact on the world comes with a net negative impact on profits, as the social efforts merely take time and money away from the core revenue-generating functions of the company. The right-hand side represents the wishful thinking that positive impact unreservedly comes with a net positive impact on profit, the fantasy that good intentions are enough, and that the market will magically reward those actors with the purest motives.

Correlation (Profit, Impact) <<0   **This book**   Correlation (Profit, Impact) >>0
Pure public goods   Business case strong

FIGURE 1.2

I reject both of these perspectives. Either can be true depending on the circumstance. Some companies can move toward the right side of the figure, but not all. As the world economy carves out a path toward closer alignment between business and societal interests, it is up to all of us to shape that journey. This book provides an answer to what differentiates the successes from the failures.

WHY, HOW, AND IN WHAT WAYS ESG AFFECTS YOU

Fundamentally, *Purpose + Profit* is about and for people—entrepreneurs, young professionals, midlevel managers, senior executives, investors, and others—who are operating across the spectrum of social impact, from serving their workforces and local communities to addressing the environment, inequality, and other global issues, and doing it not just to make them feel better, but as drivers of business success. The book aims to help us all figure out *why* doing good is leading some companies to new heights, *how* these companies are doing it, and *what* you need to understand in order to take advantage of what has become a powerful new alignment in society.

Purpose + Profit is backed by more than fifty research papers and field studies that my coauthors (at Harvard and elsewhere) and I have conducted over the past decade, as well as practical experiences that I have accumulated as an entrepreneur, board director, and investor.

I wrote this book for doers, for people who believe that, as entrepreneurs, professionals, investors, or employees at any level or stage of their careers, they can deploy their skills and knowledge to improve society. It took a long time for me to convince people that

ESG factors matter in business. If I did not think these issues were absolutely worth bringing to the forefront and could truly change the world, I would have given up long before the tide turned and moved on to a research area far more straightforward and broadly accepted.

What is so extraordinary about the alignment of purpose and profit is that it heightens everything I love about business, not just from an organizational and societal perspective, but from a personal one as well. When your work is fulfilling and rewarding to you as an individual, you work harder and, inevitably, you innovate. The world gets better cars, better coffee, better building supplies, better everything, and the increased productivity shows up in the bottom line. Despite worrying about factors that go well beyond pure profit, you end up more profitable in the end. This is an extraordinary example of a virtuous cycle that exists now as never before in history. By the end of this book, you should be able to look at your career and the world through a new lens, convinced that there is no better time to pursue your dreams and see them pay off in the world. There is a path for us all to lift up the world through business. It comes down to the power of combining purpose and profit.

PART I

Alignment: Creating Opportunity for Greater Corporate Purpose

Chapter One

THE BUSINESS OF BEING IN BUSINESS: WHAT HAS CHANGED

In the beginning of 2016, I found myself talking to automobile executives about climate change, specifically about how electrification was a megatrend that was going to reshape their industry. They dismissed the idea as something much too far in the future to consider; they believed it was unlikely to affect them before 2030 or even beyond. They laughed when I mentioned Tesla, saying there was no way Tesla would ever be able to build reliable cars at scale, let alone make an impact on their business. Edzard Reuter, former chair of the car giant Daimler, called Tesla "a joke that can't be taken seriously compared to the great car companies of Germany."[1]

Just a few years later, everyone is trying to catch up to Tesla. The company is worth more than many of its competitors—Toyota, Volkswagen, Daimler, General Motors, BMW, Honda, Hyundai, Fiat Chrysler, and Ford—not just individually, but combined.[2] Tesla has done this while remaining focused on purpose, not just profit. Elon Musk can at times be an erratic entrepreneur, but it is hard to doubt his commitment to innovation, developing real-world solutions, and making a difference when it comes to climate change.

Purpose isn't just for entrepreneurs starting new companies. Purpose is at the core of Satya Nadella's transformation of Microsoft from a company once written off as irrelevant, incapable of innovating, and doomed to fail into, for the second time in its history, one of the most valuable companies in the world. Nadella is driven to infuse purpose into everything Microsoft does, insisting that the company is motivated by one goal: to enable people to improve their lives through technology. He used that core value to reinvent the company's culture, restore its spirit of innovation, and help make the tech industry more inclusive. On the innovation side, Nadella has done this by moving the company's focus beyond just the Windows operating system to new areas such as cloud computing. Regarding inclusivity, he has increased the diversity of the talent inside Microsoft in terms of race and gender, and has made expanding opportunities for employees a key piece of his philosophy.

"I always go back to that social contract of our company with the world around us," Nadella says. "You can't exist if all you're doing is benefiting yourself. . . . Profit [comes] because of the larger surplus you're creating around you."[3] The company, ranked America's most JUST company by the nonprofit JUST Capital three years in a row (2019–2021), has become a leader in efforts to protect the environment and strengthen democracy around the world.[4] A powerful lesson from the Microsoft example is that legacy companies can be reinvented for their own good and for the good of society. Their past is not their destiny. Leaders have considerable agency to define their own future and the future of their organizations.

"When we talk about our mission of empowering every person and every organization on the planet to achieve more," Nadella told CNET, "[it] can't be just a set of words. It has to in some sense capture the very essence of who we are in all of the decisions we make, in the products we create and how we show up with our customers."[5]

BEHIND THE CORPORATE MAKEOVER: PURPOSE-DRIVEN MOTIVATORS

Young and old companies are transforming themselves and transforming their industries through something broader than merely seeking profit. I believe that understanding what is going on comes down to a simple question:

Why do people go into business?

I ask that question to my Harvard Business School students, and the answers I get depend almost entirely on *how* I ask it. If I ask it in the abstract, as I just did, "Why do people—other people, people in the news, people whose minds and motivations you can only hypothesize about—go into business?" then the answer is easy: to make money. That is the caricature of a businessperson, but it's more than just a caricature. It's the baseline assumption and expectation. If you go back to economist Milton Friedman and his incredibly influential 1970 op-ed piece in the *New York Times*, "A Friedman Doctrine—The Social Responsibility of Business Is to Increase Its Profits," it's the imperative.[6] Friedman argued that the business of business is business, and the sole aim of a corporate leader must be to maximize profits, social impact, and all other factors be damned.

However, if I frame the question as "Why do *you* want to go into business?" my students' answers are generally very different. They tell me that they are motivated by the challenge to create—to create products and services that will satisfy and delight consumers, to create jobs, and to create a life for themselves filled with intellectual challenge, rewarding professional relationships, high-performing teams, and societal impact. Of course they want to make money, because that gives them the ability to buy the goods and services that they want in their own lives, but for most people, the motivation to go into business is not just about maximizing profitability. That isn't what gets them up in the morning excited to start their day.

THE URGE TO MAKE A DIFFERENCE AND A PROFIT

Years ago, I met Reynir Indahl when he was working at one of the best-performing private equity firms in the world. Yet when the financial crisis hit in 2007, he felt like a prisoner of the system. It made him think hard about the problems of inequality in society, and he realized he wanted to be sure he was on the right side of the issues, creating positive outcomes instead of contributing to negative effects in the world.

Reynir eventually decided to make a change. After he visited Harvard Business School to speak to one of my classes, we had lunch, and he asked my advice about where he should go next in his career. He was passionate about making a difference, but did not feel that he could do so in his existing role. I asked him, "Why don't you start your own private equity firm?" A few months later, Reynir started Summa Equity, a private equity firm defined by its focus on environmental, social, and governance (ESG) issues, creating solutions that contribute toward the United Nations Sustainable Development Goals (no poverty, zero hunger, quality education, equality and justice, and a clean environment among them). Reynir believes companies that are taking the lead on ESG issues—such as climate change, education, and increasing the quality of life through innovations in health care—are going to see the greatest growth going forward, and that contributing to the world isn't just about getting better press or placating consumers. It's about business strategy and growth. He believes that by becoming experts in ESG, Summa could contribute to the success of these companies and make a positive impact.

I have been fortunate to be an advisor to Summa and an investor in the firm, witnessing firsthand how Reynir and his partners have built a truly purpose-driven organization. Summa Equity now has more than $1 billion under management, and, at the same time, is helping to build a more sustainable planet. In 2021, Summa exited its first investment, at the environmental solutions company Sortera, having grown revenues sevenfold over five years, and its valuation even more than that, a remarkable return.

I have seen many others like Reynir, successful people at the midpoints of their careers, realizing that they are not pursuing what really motivates them. They have decided to take a risk, do something more impactful, and attempt to make a difference. I have increasingly seen the same from people just starting out.

Jarrid Tingle, one of my former students, is an example of this phenomenon. Jarrid was raised by a single mother near Philadelphia. Only through a program for low-income families could he attend a competitive private high school, which made it possible for him to study for his undergraduate degree at the Wharton School of the University of Pennsylvania and then earn an investment banking job at Barclays.

In his late twenties, along with a few friends, he cofounded Harlem Capital Partners, a venture capital firm focused on making investments in businesses founded by minorities and women. As Jarrid has explained, he found in his research that it was harder for minority- and women-owned businesses to get funding. Those that did find success inevitably had to overcome greater challenges.

Jarrid initially struggled to raise any money at all, but ended up launching a venture fund with $40 million, giving Harlem Capital a fighting chance to reach its goal of investing in one thousand diverse founders over the next twenty years. In 2021, Harlem raised a second venture capital fund, this time for $134 million. As Jarrid said to me when we were writing a business school case on Harlem Capital after he graduated from Harvard Business School, "People thought that investing in a diverse set of entrepreneurs was impossible. We set out to prove that thinking wrong."[7] And they have.

Another former student, Tiffany Pham, is an example of the same impulse to contribute to society. Tiffany's grandmother was an entrepreneur in Vietnam, running newspapers, owning businesses, and becoming one of the first women in the country to drive a car. Tiffany, following in her grandmother's footsteps, built a career for herself in the entertainment industry.

In 2014, *Forbes* named Tiffany one of its "30 Under 30" influential people in the media industry, and that's when her life changed.

After the *Forbes* article, Tiffany was deluged by emails from young women seeking advice as they launched their own careers. As she corresponded with many of them, she realized there was a hunger felt by ambitious young women around the world, desperate for advice and opportunities. Tiffany decided to create a platform to provide just that—in the process learning to code the initial site on her own—and that platform became Mogul, a social media platform that now provides education and resources to women across the globe. The company has created a lucrative subscription-based business model connecting employers looking for diverse talent with millions of potential new employees. Tiffany counts among her clients some of the largest companies in the world.

These examples illustrate that leading with purpose—having business motivation grounded not only in potential profit but also driven by a broader mission—can be a road toward success and fulfillment, and that people at every stage of their careers can be operating with these ideas in mind.

SUSTAINABILITY AT THE HIGHEST LEVELS

These same issues, of course, play out even for the world's largest businesses. There is the famous case of Paul Polman, the former CEO of Unilever, one of the world's largest consumer goods companies. Unilever has more than four hundred associated brands (including Ben & Jerry's ice cream, Dove cleaning products, Hellman's mayonnaise, Knorr soup, Lipton tea, and many more) and is the largest producer of soap in the world.

"The two biggest challenges that need to be addressed are climate change and inequality," according to Polman.[8] "Anytime you know that you're polluting and putting carbon in the air, someone else is going to die. Anytime you know you're wasting food, someone else is going to die. It is our problem. We are living on the same planet. If we don't find a way to live in harmony with our fellow citizens, it's not going to work."[9]

Each year, Unilever releases its Annual Report, which includes an accounting of the company's achievements in addressing some of society's most challenging problems.[10] The report proclaims the company's commitment to improving the health and hygiene of billions of people around the world, saving our environment, creating a more inclusive set of business opportunities, empowering women, and more.

The company's plans and actions are not charity; it uses its sustainability goals to grow its business, creating a stronger bond with both customers and employees in the process. Unilever's stock price more than doubled under Polman's tenure. As the company writes on its website, "We have long known that growth and sustainability are not in conflict."[11] In 2018, Unilever's Sustainable Living Brands, the brands furthest ahead on the company's journey toward meeting its goals, grew 69 percent faster than the rest of the portfolio.[12] These sustainable brands aren't sacrifices the company is making for the good of the planet—they are the difference-makers driving the company to success.

"We believe the evidence is clear and compelling that brands with purpose grow," said Alan Jope, who replaced Polman as Unilever CEO in 2019. "Purpose creates relevance for a brand, it drives talkability, builds penetration and reduces price elasticity. In fact, we believe this so strongly that we are prepared to commit that in the future, every Unilever brand will be a brand with purpose."[13]

THE ROAD TO DOING GOOD: BEYOND A SINGLE FOCUS ON PROFIT

Stories like Reynir's, Jarrid's, Tiffany's, and Paul's—people in very different industries, at very different stages of their careers, doing different things with completely different missions, but with the underlying goal of making big differences in people's lives—are why I have such a great love for business and its possibilities. The leaps society has made in terms of the sheer improvements in all of our lives, from being able to travel, to communicate, even to taste an amazing range of foods from around the globe, are incredible. They have come about because business has been able to create solutions to problems we did not even know we had. From curing diseases to simply creating a great new flavor of coffee, the range of things that business has brought us is extraordinary.

The reality is that many businesses focus on far more than profits. They engage in efforts to address societal problems, to improve inequality, to rescue the climate, and to fight poverty. They do this in part because businesses are made up of individuals, who want to wake up each morning believing that they are doing good for the world, creating for others and not merely enriching themselves. They also do this because, as in the cases I've already mentioned, it can be very good business.

Milton Friedman's perspective that the sole responsibility and focus of business should be profit, with no attention paid to how that profit is created, reflected the time in which he was writing. In the setting of the Cold War, his goal was to show that open and free markets were superior to the government controls of the Soviet Union. He worried that giving managers permission to chase anything but profits would open the door to corruption and enable them to enrich themselves at the expense of investors.

Perhaps Friedman was even more worried that the cure would be worse than the problem, and that allowing managers to make decisions with social welfare in mind would turn the market process into a political process. A move toward central planning might lead to government control over the allocation of scarce resources, subverting competition, private ownership, and eventually individual freedom.

I sympathize with these types of concerns. Having grown up in Greece in the 1980s and '90s, living under governments that exerted strong control over business, with damaging consequences for the economy and the welfare of its citizens, I have seen many of the things that Friedman worried about. But Friedman was also acting under a set of assumptions that have either changed over time or been proven wrong.

First, fifty years ago there was little visibility into corporate behavior, and no way for outsiders to track much beyond the stock price. Employees or customers with a preference for companies doing good in the world had no real way to express that preference. The information simply did not exist. We are now creating accountability structures in society (ESG metrics and impact-weighted accounting work that we will examine further in this book) so that these efforts can be observed, tracked, and analyzed.

Without this data, the assumption was that mission-oriented companies were trading profits for purpose, and that, in a fully functioning market, those companies would fail. Armed now with relevant data, we can see that purpose-oriented companies often don't fail. Purpose-driven enterprises that genuinely create value for society do better, and the effect only increases over time. This is why we've seen the rise of everything from B Corps—small organizations that have become officially certified by the nonprofit B Lab (more about them in chapter two)—to large, purpose-driven companies like Unilever, Natura &Co, and many more.

Another set of assumptions concerned the idea of fully functioning markets with no external consequences, no information asymmetry between buyers and sellers, and no ability for a firm to capture the political process and influence policies, prices, and regulations. These assumptions, common for decades, have proven to be wrong, and the costs of getting them wrong keep increasing. Environmental degradation has grown out of control; we struggle with persistent inequality of opportunity across groups of different socioeconomic backgrounds; the wage gap between the richest and poorest in society is growing; there is an increasing prevalence of chronic illnesses such as cardiovascular disease and diabetes; and on and on. These problems are not independent of business, and it was wrong to ever assume that they were.

Today, only about 20 percent of all greenhouse gas emissions are subject to some kind of price—there is no universal carbon tax—and companies do have tremendous influence and power in our governmental systems, from oil and gas companies influencing energy pricing to financial services firms influencing banking regulations to pharmaceutical companies influencing drug pricing. Between dark money and broader issues with campaign financing, in the United States at least, it is clear that the political system can be captured in ways that were not driving people's thinking until recently.

One more major weakness I find in the old thinking is the assumption that there are only two relevant people in business: the CEO leading the firm and the investor looking for profits. This is a simplistic view of the world. The reality is that most people aren't CEOs, but still have a huge interest in the direction that a company is pursuing. People go into the business world—at every level—because, just as my students insist, they think they can make a difference, provide value to the marketplace, and live according to their values.

Unfortunately, the legacy of these historical assumptions leaves those who care about issues beyond immediate profit worrying that they seem weak or soft, or lack commitment to the reality of the marketplace. This plays out all the time in conversations I have with students and recent graduates. One former student, who was working for a very successful company, told me that she hesitated to bring up issues about how the firm could more effectively change the world, provide better products, or take larger social issues into account when advising clients because she worried about being seen as someone who wasn't motivated by the "right" things.

As much as she was trying to fight against it, she still felt she was supposed to act like Gordon Gekko—the *Wall Street* character played by Michael Douglas, operating under a "greed is good" mantra. She imagined that she would be outcompeted if she let herself be distracted by other concerns. I did not push back when we talked. Instead, I asked her if those people trying to diminish her efforts to do good were in fact the most successful ones around her, or the people she looked up to at work.

When she reflected on this—and when I did, too—we both realized that the people who express these ideas, who put others down for thinking about the societal impact of the work they do, who seem driven by nothing more than pure greed, are rarely if ever the best performers in an organization. They are not the ones she or I wanted to model ourselves after, or the ones with whom we had worked most effectively.

The question, then, isn't about how we ignore the "soft" issues, stop caring, and move past our concerns about our impact on the world. Rather, it's about turning those issues into challenges for which we can provide solutions through entrepreneurial efforts. How do we make diversity not just something we give lip service to, but, as with Harlem Capital, actually use it to create added business value? How do we turn environmental concerns, strong ethics, broader product access, and more into opportunities for growth, to drive new products and new markets, rather than obstacles we have to overcome?

Questions like these are critical as we think about the intersection of purpose and profit, and the answers can make or break a business. In the chapters to come, I intend to make the case that these questions get to the heart of what the business of business needs to be to find success in the world right now.

EXPANDING THE BUSINESS OF BUSINESS

In August 2019, the Business Roundtable, an organization consisting of 181 top global CEOs, including the leaders of companies like Apple, Walmart, Amazon, American Express, BP, ExxonMobil, and Goldman Sachs, issued an open letter that repudiated the view that the business of business is merely the chase for profit. It declared a commitment to delivering value to customers, employees, and the country.

"We foster diversity and inclusion, dignity and respect," the letter read. "We are dedicated to serving as good partners to the other companies, large and small, that help us meet our missions. . . . We respect the people in our communities and protect the environment by embracing sustainable practices across our businesses."[14]

It's no surprise that this letter did not lead to massive, instant change at the signatory companies, nor did this endorsement suddenly make things easy for everyone who was trying to act with purpose in mind. As I said in the introduction, engineering these changes wasn't a trivial task. At the same time that Paul Polman was receiving glowing press throughout the world for Unilever's sustainability efforts, David Crane, the CEO of another Fortune 500 company, NRG Energy, a coal-based power generator—the second-largest power generator in the United States—publicly committed to reducing his company's carbon use by 50 percent by 2030 and 90 percent by 2050. He was set to invest NRG's coal profits into renewable energy and transform his company from one of the world's largest corporate polluters into a green giant.

Crane launched the strategy in 2014, announcing, in words that could have come from Paul Polman's mouth, "The day is coming when our children sit us down in our dotage, look us straight in the eye, with an acute sense of betrayal and disappointment in theirs, and whisper to us, 'You knew . . . and you didn't do anything about it. Why?'"[15]

The result? NRG's stock price declined, Crane was fired less than two years after announcing the green initiatives, and, as the company returned to its polluting ways, the stock price shot back up. NRG's efforts to travel the same road as Unilever became a much-talked-about failure. "[T]he thing I struggle with most," Crane told Greentech Media, "is that I thought my special contribution to the [climate] cause was showing how a fossil fuel company can become a green company, but by getting fired and not getting there, I've sent the opposite message: if you think you can transform your company and get rewarded for it—you can't."[16]

NRG's story is proof that the business of business has not yet transformed the world into a capitalist utopia. Nevertheless, it is still the case that statements like the one by the Business Roundtable are indicative of a change. It's very hard to find a successful company today—or, honestly, even an unsuccessful one—that is willing to come out and say that it is completely ignoring these issues. Even NRG Energy now trumpets sustainability success on its website.[17] People might say that this is just about reputation, but that is only part of the point. The forces aligning these factors are so strong that there are no companies willing to come out and say that they don't matter. The companies taking the lead on these issues, doing more than the minimum, and going further than just acknowledging their importance, are finding that they are the issues enabling success. The Business Roundtable statement is about survival—you can't survive without at least a nod toward social good. The fact is that, increasingly, success is emerging from companies that fully embrace these issues and make them a priority.

The transparency of the workplace has helped tremendously. Companies can't hide things as they once did. To some degree, transparency has moved too far in the other direction; there is information overload and a tremendous amount of noise in the background. It means that you cannot hide negative impacts. If something terrible is happening in your supply chain in a distant country, people will find out. This simply wasn't the case in the 1970s and '80s. We went two decades where virtually the only company that received attacks along these lines was Nike, which was forced to make massive changes in favor of human rights. Now, detection is far more likely. It is a much more transparent world. (I will cover this topic in more detail in chapter three.)

At the same time, as societies have grown richer, issues of social justice have become much more important to individuals. Human rights, and the costs of not respecting them, are becoming much more salient. It is, to some extent, a generational issue. Young people really do care about the state of the world. I remember a conversation with one leader who expressed personal skepticism about ESG issues, but said he was forced to act, because all his employees would revolt if he did not. My research on this topic, which we'll explore in chapter two, shows that employees at every level matter tremendously when it comes to companies taking these issues seriously. It is the whole workforce, not just the C-suite executives, that is mobilizing companies to drive these issues forward.

Efforts focused on larger societal issues show their benefit on many different levels: public relations, innovation as a company, and, in a sometimes-overlooked example, recruiting and retaining the best people, making sure they care enough about the firm's mission that they work their hardest and bring their best every day.

The alternative—keeping mission and purpose out of the workplace—ends up starving business of an incredible amount of talent and motivation. I see it so clearly in my own work, not just as a professor and researcher, but as a practitioner who has built consulting and technology firms and works directly with business leaders around the world. Passion and purpose drive innovation; when it is just about the money, jobs become uncompelling and empty. Rather than making talented people excited to pursue their entrepreneurial ideas, a single-minded focus on profits puts them in a narrow box from which they look to escape.

THE PROOF IS IN THE RESULTS

Where this leaves us is with an extraordinarily virtuous cycle of sustainability and the core of the argument I'll continue to make in the rest of this book. Purpose-driven companies have better outcomes—in part because there are incredible ways to use sustainability factors as business drivers, motivating more innovation and informing decisions about products and services, and also in part because companies that care about these issues inspire employees who care and who are willing to invest more and work harder. It can often be costlier to the individual to go all in on the mission and purpose of their work: just look at Reynir Indahl, leaving a top-performing firm to take on unnecessary risk. At the same time, it changes the benefits. The rewards to individuals are much higher when they feel proud of what they are contributing to each day.

Steve Jobs said in his Stanford commencement address in 2005, "[T]he only way to be truly satisfied is to do what you believe is great work. And the only way to do great work is to love what you do."[18] That is why being purpose-driven is important, and why the business of business has to be more than just business.

A LOOK FORWARD: A NEW GENERATION

In the next chapter, I will delve deeper into how attitudes and behaviors have shifted over the past fifty years and how today's young people—the "Impact Generation"—are driving many of the decisions companies are making along sustainability lines. As both consumers and employees, they are unwilling to ignore or accept bad behavior to the extent that people may have in the past. Combined with the societal realization that business may have a larger purpose than just profit, these personal impulses to do more, and contribute more, are driving much of the change we see in today's world.

Chapter Two

THE IMPACT OF
THE "IMPACT GENERATION"

Most of my students aren't old enough to remember a time when, as both consumers and employees, we didn't have nearly as much choice as we do today. To take a simple example, I can remember as a child growing up in Greece going to the market and, if you wanted milk, there was one choice—milk. Now, even the smallest mini-mart invariably has dozens of options, from conventional to organic, full fat, low fat, no fat, soy milk, almond milk, coconut milk, oat milk, hemp milk, vanilla-flavored, sweetened or unsweetened. And if there aren't enough choices in your local store, you can almost certainly find exactly what you are looking for online; that is, if the vendor hasn't already targeted you with an ad on your favorite social media platform.

On the employment side, I remember seeing help wanted ads in newspapers. The number of ways to find a job opening was incredibly limited compared to today's world of LinkedIn and the endless range of online job boards, mailing lists, and Facebook groups for virtually every industry or profession—not to mention the explosion in remote work that allows people to expand their job search worldwide. Plus, the amount of information you might have about a company before you take a job has massively increased compared to just a generation ago. From sites like Glassdoor, which allow you to read employee reviews, to the

simple ability to look at websites and news articles, the amount
of transparency is extraordinary.

All of this choice enables people to pursue and express all kinds
of preferences in ways that weren't previously available, as well as
align their consumption and their employment with their values,
something previously impossible. If you care about the environment, you can choose products from environmentally conscious
companies, and seek to work for a company that shares that mission. If you are a company that cares about a particular cause, you
have many ways (through social media and other signaling) to
announce it to the world, and recruit customers and employees
who are drawn to that purpose as well.

The data I've collected, from about half a million employees
across more than four hundred large organizations, shows that
purpose-driven companies—those that score high on a measure I
call purpose-clarity—perform substantially better than their competitors, with significant, positive risk-adjusted stock returns of
about 6 percent annually. This may be in part because they are
attracting better workers, or because their workers are motivated
to work harder when they believe in the purpose of their job. It
may be in part because customers see those same signals and would
like to do business with those companies or buy their products, and
are even willing to pay a premium to do so. Purpose and success
are shown by the research to be closely aligned. We are acting in
greater accordance with our values when it comes to our consumption and our employment.

In this chapter, I will explore consumer and employee empower-
ment along these lines through four clear societal trends:

- Increased availability of *choice,*
- Increased *transparency* (visibility) of corporate behavior,
- Increased opportunity for employees and consumers to express
  their *voice,* and

- The increasing importance of *value* (human and social capital) as compared to physical resources.

This is illustrated in figure 2.1. I'll conclude by diving into the data on corporate purpose and show how these trends can pay off for companies.

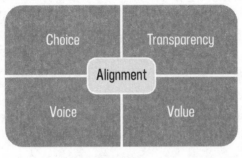

FIGURE 2.1

CHOICE AND VARIETY:
MORE MILKS, MORE JEANS, MORE BANKS

In 1970, there were four types of milk, five possible sizes for a television screen, sixteen brands of mineral water, 160 breakfast cereals, and 339 newspapers. By 2012, those numbers had ballooned: more than fifty types of milk, forty-three television-screen sizes, 195 brands of mineral water, 4,945 cereals, and more than five thousand newspapers.[1] We live in a world of extraordinary choice. Partly this is due to globalization—the increased ability to distribute products around the world with lowered barriers when it comes to delivery and price. However, technology has not only enabled us to purchase things from more distant sources, it has also helped us to know about them. The internet has virtually eliminated the cost of obtaining knowledge, and social media has transformed the ability of companies, even tiny ones, to advertise to increasingly precise slices of the population. Coupled with an increased culture of entrepreneurship worldwide, lower costs to start businesses across all dimensions, lower costs to find new customers, and lower costs to manufacture goods, the result has been huge increases in consumer choice and product variety.

Companies like Kellogg's understood that there was an audience for natural and organic foods beyond their core offerings, which is why in the year 2000 they bought the brand Kashi and grew it into a megabrand with more than ninety product offerings. Airbnb expanded the range of what people could find in a hotel accommodation, with an endless range of unique places to stay and the possibility of booking local activities with hosts.

But choice isn't just about superficial preferences. In the absence of choice, customers are unable to express their preferences or influence corporate behavior. If the only option is to buy products from a bad company—on whatever dimension you choose to define "bad"—they will. Instead, now consumers have far more ability to match their idiosyncratic needs in whatever category they choose, whether it's design, taste, or issues closer to the heart of ESG-related concerns like social consciousness or environmental sustainability. It's not just about offering options—it's about enabling consumers to feel empowered to do business with companies they perceive as aligned with their values, and providing products that align with them as well.

That's why even in unexpected industries like banking, there are examples such as Aspiration, a values-based bank that promises to be "a new kind of financial partner that puts our customers and their conscience first."[2] It does this by offering socially conscious, sustainable money management, promising that deposits "won't fund fossil fuel exploration or production," offering cash back on purchases from other socially conscious businesses, and giving a percentage of their fees to charitable causes.

The consumer goods company Seventh Generation, owned by Unilever, produces plant-based cleaning products and issues an annual Corporate Consciousness Report to the public, demonstrating the company's commitment to sustainability.[3] Seventh Generation gives consumers who want their household projects to align with their values a real choice in the marketplace. The car company Tesla provides an annual impact report.[4] The alternative milk company Oatly trumpets the superior efficiency of oats over dairy, giving space in the nutrition facts on its website to announce that Oatly generates 80 percent fewer greenhouse-gas emissions and uses 60 percent less energy than the producers of cow's milk.[5] These are companies doing their best to expand consumer options and give people a way to connect their beliefs and their purchases.

At PepsiCo, former CEO Indra Nooyi nearly lost her job fighting to move the company in a more sustainable direction and give customers healthier food and beverage options. Her "profits with purpose" push toward healthier products was derided as "feel-good nonsense" according to *Business Insider*, and was ridiculed by analysts.[6] Nevertheless, Nooyi saw the future and sensed that the world was moving in the direction where concerns like these mattered to consumers. Moving the company toward healthier products resulted in a doubling of the share price during her tenure.[7]

These are just a few examples of the many—and there are many—to choose from. The data shows that these kinds of proclamations make a real difference to consumers. As a society, our tolerance for bad actors—our willingness to accept companies that don't offer choices along environmentally and socially beneficial dimensions—is far lower than it used to be. We expect more nutritious food, products that don't damage the world, and more corporate concern for social issues. One study found that customers of clothing retailer Gap chose ethically labeled products over those without similar labels if given an option. Denim jean labels with information about a program to reduce water pollution in manufacturing increased sales by 8 percent, for female shoppers specifically, and an experiment found that clothing with fair labor standards on the label led to higher sales.[8]

Indeed, at an event where we both spoke, Richard Edelman, CEO of Edelman, a leading global public relations firm, told the audience that consumers are increasingly seeking to align their purchases with brands they trust. As a businessperson, there is one important thing to remember: customers are smart. According to the Edelman Trust Barometer, a survey about the sources of information most trusted by people around the globe, half of consumers across eight countries feel that brands use societal issues as a marketing ploy to sell more products.[9] Consumers want reality, not just image. That helps explain why we now see detailed reports on so many corporate websites, why companies provide data to back up their claims, and why these trends have stuck and grown over the past generation and not simply been a flash in the pan.

CHOICE: NOT JUST CONSUMERS. *INDEED*; THINK WORKERS

Options have dramatically expanded not just for consumers, but for employees as well. Just as with consumers, if you are a potential employee and the only possible job is at a bad employer, you will inevitably have to take it. But now, expectations and desires are much broader—and the marketplace provides many more options to exercise choice than ever before. Many of my students tell me that they cannot imagine having a job that's just a job. They want more than that—they want fulfillment and purpose—and insist that any business not prioritizing social contribution is going to be left behind, unable to keep star employees or recruit anyone of quality.

Some of this desire comes from the fact that the personal and professional are more mixed up than ever in many people's lives. While you once were able to leave your job at the office, the work environment—through remote work, smartphones, and the 24/7 culture we live in—now penetrates just about every aspect of our lives. Many companies offer benefits to employees that blur the line even further, with tech companies often leading the way by providing on-site gyms, free food, sports teams, transportation, social events, and even on-campus living in some cases. There have always been "company towns" like Pullman, Illinois, in the 1800s, with corporate housing and amenities for employees of the Pullman Palace Car Company, or Hershey, Pennsylvania, in the early 1900s. Some of these hybrid work/living situations treated workers well, and some of them were far less utopian, but even at their peak in the United States, company towns only housed an estimated 3 percent of the working population.[10] Now, the number of people whose work-life balance is impossibly blurred is far greater.

A report by National Car Rental puts unsurprising numbers on this trend. Sixty-five percent of survey respondents said it was unrealistic to try to draw a line between their work and personal lives. Workers reported answering job-related emails after work hours almost four days in an average week, taking work calls from home three days a week, and taking personal calls at the office, or working on personal projects there, almost as often. Beyond that, business travel has morphed into what now is known as "bleisure" travel, with 61 percent of survey respondents incorporating leisure activities into business trips, and 50 percent of executives extending business trips into leisure travel.[11]

All of this means that workers can't leave their values at home when they go to the office. They expect to find employers whose priorities align with their own. Fortunately, expanded choice allows them to do so. The start-up revolution has led to an increasing number of people and amount of capital going to disruptive new organizations. (For instance, the percentage of MBAs graduating from top schools and joining start-ups has increased from a percentage in the low single digits a decade ago to more than a quarter of the graduating classes today.) Greater access to capital and financing (with the growth of the venture capital industry) has meant there are more employers, just from a numbers perspective; in particular, there are more fast-growing, smaller organizations that may have an increased openness to new, progressive ways of thinking compared to established giants.

Beyond the total number, there is also increased choice of employers thanks to technology. Globalization, the opening up of European borders, and the decreased cost of transportation allow far more employee mobility; remote work allows people to decouple where they live and where they work; and the internet has enabled the discovery of job opportunities in a way that was unimaginable not long ago.

The online job platform Indeed receives more than two hundred million visits per month, and claims to have delivered 65 percent of all hires in the United States found using online sources in 2016.[12] LinkedIn has more than twenty million open jobs listed on its site, with three million more posted each month in the United States.[13] But it is not just finding a new job that is easier because of the internet. There is also the upskilling component that the internet enables, increasing the number of career options for many workers. LinkedIn Learning, with video courses in software, creative, and business skills, has seventeen million users,[14] and coding boot camps have popped up—online and offline—to teach computer programming and other tech skills, graduating an estimated twenty-three thousand new software developers in 2019.[15]

I see the results of increased mobility and choice not only in the decisions my students make, but also in my own role as an entrepreneur. I cofounded KKS Advisors, a strategy and consulting firm with a mission to help businesses make decisions for the long term, taking into account the same kinds of environmental, social, and governance factors discussed throughout this book. Over the years this mission made it possible for us to attract highly skilled employees in our London, Boston, and Athens offices. I know these people had many other choices, including larger firms that could afford to pay higher salaries and provide amazing opportunities simply because of their size and the range of companies they work with.

As my cofounder, Sakis Kotsantonis, put it, "We can't have the best sales pitch on every dimension, but when it comes to doing work with meaning and purpose, we do believe we can compete with anyone." Sakis's story is itself a testament to that. After graduating with a doctorate in engineering from Imperial College London, one of the top universities in the world, instead of continuing the work he was familiar with in the world of science, dealing with metals and fuel cells, he chose to pursue a career path full of long hours and deep uncertainty. After working at IBM and Deloitte, he started KKS, a professional-services firm with a mission to infuse sustainability into business. Sakis did this because he wanted to make a difference, and his passion has given us a real edge, enabling us to hire and retain true superstars. As a result, our offices have attracted top employees from Finland, Spain, France, Germany, Italy, India, and the United States, all people who moved to pursue their goals at a workplace that empowered them to have an impact.

TRANSPARENCY AND INFORMATION: THE VISIBILITY OF CORPORATE B-HAVIOR

All of this increased choice is powered largely by the growth in reliable information about company behavior and the increased transparency of that information. The nonprofit B Lab certifies B Corps, companies that meet the highest standards of social and environmental performance.[16] As the B Corp site explains, "Society's most challenging problems cannot be solved by government and nonprofits alone. The B Corp community works toward reduced inequality, lower levels of poverty, a healthier environment, stronger communities, and the creation of more high quality jobs with dignity and purpose."[17]

There are more than 3,500 companies in 150 industries and 74 countries that have chosen to pursue certification. These range from relatively small businesses, like Animikii, a web services company in British Columbia, Canada, to Danone, the multinational food conglomerate (Dannon yogurt, Evian water, Silk alternative milk products, and many other brands) with more than $29 billion in annual revenue and more than 100,000 employees.

The crowdfunding company Kickstarter is a great example of a B Corp focused around a mission of altruism. A few years ago, reports *Fast Company*, the founders decided that they had reached their financial goals and that "the company should exist for two reasons: It should continue to innovate and build products that improved the lives of artists, and they should lead a new movement of corporate governance."[18] The company operates with multiple goals in mind—not just profit, but also making life better for employees and for users of the site. In 2017, *Fast Company* reported that the company was paying its executives "less than five times their average employee, compared to the 95-times industry average," along with going above most companies' typical efforts to increase diversity, in this case hiring all of its interns from nonprofits devoted to the diversity mission.[19]

When the idea of B Corps started, few imagined that it would take off. The idea that investors would finance companies that were publicly announcing a commitment to something beyond profit was unthinkable—until it wasn't. B Lab faced much resistance, but the marketplace was ready for it, and employees and customers were eager to have the stamp of approval, validating the efforts that a company was making.

B Corp certification allows a company to signal its commitment to ESG issues, and it is an important signal that many find meaningful. It is also the case that our world now has many more ways of detecting and communicating corporate behavior along these lines. It used to be impossible to know how companies were performing with respect to these issues. The metrics did not even exist, making it unthinkable to require companies to communicate about any kind of ESG-related performance. We'll dive more into the metrics in chapter three; the important point here is that they exist, and they are becoming ubiquitous through organizations like the

Global Reporting Initiative and the Sustainability Accounting Standards Board, which have fought for high-quality disclosure of these types of efforts from companies around the world. Thousands of companies report on their environmental, social, and governance data—from fewer than 20 percent of S&P 500 companies in 2011 to almost 90 percent by 2019—and if your company doesn't, the implication is that you have something to hide.

The forces are so powerful in favor of good behavior along these measures that it is far more often about companies looking for ways to signal good behavior than about hiding problems. In chapter three, we'll also talk about the lack of secrets. Companies can't hide their pollution, sweatshops, child labor, and internal scandals the way they could in the past, thanks to increased reporting requirements, heightened interest from the press, and the ubiquity of social media. However, in most cases, it's not even about trying to hide anything. Instead, it is about companies wanting to share information, proud to announce it, because they know that their customers, employees, and investors want to see it.

Beyond B Corp status, there are several alternative corporate models many organizations have adopted to signal their commitment to ESG issues. These include the Public Benefit Corporation, a form Kickstarter adopted in 2015, building even further on its B Corp status, and the Social Purpose Corporation, which started in California in 2012. (A number of other states have also adopted it.) An SPC provides legal protection for managers to consider environmental and social issues in their corporate decisions and requires the articles of incorporation to state a social or environmental purpose for the company. Around the world, there are many similar corporate forms available, including Societa Benefit in Italy, Community Interest Companies in the United Kingdom, and Community Contribution Companies in British Columbia, Canada.

Even for companies that won't go as far as pursuing B Corp certification or changing their formal corporate structure, there is a range of other ways they can signal to the market that they care about these issues. First, they can stop the practice of quarterly earnings guidance (distinct from quarterly earnings *reporting*), which promotes short-term, profit-focused thinking rather than long-term, strategic aims around social welfare. They can adopt what is known as the integrated guidance framework, incorporating forward-looking information around ESG issues into regular investor communications, in order to effectively communicate long-term goals to the public. They can produce integrated reports, like those favored by the International Integrated Reporting Council, and they can also signal internally, and to prospective hires, by aligning performance metrics with purpose.

These are all relatively formal ways that companies can signal their commitment to ESG issues. There are also more informal signaling mechanisms. At the most basic level, consumers, employees, and investors can learn about company priorities simply by looking at their websites. From small companies to large ones, you can almost pick one at random and find language on its website about the company's broader societal mission and purpose, and efforts the company is taking along those lines. Few would associate a telecommunications provider like, say, Verizon, with the idea of operating with purpose, but it announces proudly on its site a commitment to making the world a better place: "We're committed to a low carbon future. . . . We're committed to reskilling and upskilling those most vulnerable in the future economy. . . . We believe in supporting neighbors, and building community."[20]

Language like this would likely have been criticized in the past for diverting attention from the core business and wasting potential shareholder profits. And while some of it can merely be cheap talk—"purpose washing," which I'll discuss in just a bit—the fact that virtually all companies now feel compelled to make these kinds of statements shows how the need to showcase positive societal impact has become a survival issue.

VOICE AND ACTIVISM:
THE POWER OF CONSUMERS AND EMPLOYEES

The evidence that consumers and employees care deeply about these issues goes beyond simply wanting to know what companies are doing, and beyond the idea that ESG factors influence the choices people make. We are also seeing a tremendous increase in employee and consumer activism. Employees have always fought for their rights. They have organized in unions, sought collective bargaining agreements, and gone on strike when demands were not met. Still, when we think of striking workers, it is the people at the bottom of the hierarchy, the factory workers, the hourly staff, the people with limited choices and limited opportunities, whom we typically have in mind. What is different now is that the employees demanding action aren't necessarily the ones at the bottom of the hierarchy, and their demands go beyond their own working conditions to how their companies are treating others or treating the world.

At Amazon in 2019, more than eighty-seven hundred workers signed a letter asking the company to do better in its efforts to fight climate change.[21] They formed a group, Amazon Employees for Climate Justice, and organized a walkout, prompting the company to unveil a Climate Pledge, promising to become carbon-neutral by the year 2040. At Google, there is a growing movement by employees— often employees making hundreds of thousands of dollars a year—to push the company for progress on several ethical and environmental issues. The *Los Angeles Times* took a deep look at employee activism at tech companies in 2019, writing about this "new strain of worker activism, one whose practitioners are as preoccupied with the social impact of the multibillion-dollar companies that employ them as they are with their own work conditions."[22]

It's not just tech companies. Employees at the furniture company Wayfair walked out in 2019 when they learned that the firm had sold $200,000 worth of goods to the contractor running a government detention center in Texas.[23]

There is also the case of the pharmaceutical giant Merck, which understood the concerns of this new generation of employees and decided to be proactive about becoming the kind of company that its workers could believe in. When talking about the company's development of a vaccine for Ebola, CEO Ken Frazier said to investors in 2018: "Why does a company like Merck develop an Ebola vaccine? There is essentially no commercial market for an Ebola vaccine . . . [no] populations that are likely to create immediate financial value for Merck. But I can tell you, it creates tremendous business value just based on the reaction that our employees have."[24]

"In our scientific organization," Frazier continued, "it would have been impossible to say to those scientists who had the capability of doing something, we won't go there because we don't see a robust commercial market. And I think that's part of . . . having a purpose-driven organization."[25]

Employees care not only about their own working conditions, but also about their employer's actions in the world, and how their company is contributing to (or hurting) the causes employees feel deeply about. This is not typical employee behavior, and the fact that in some cases it has moved companies to change policies or make different choices is extraordinary when considering how we think about corporate behavior over the course of history. In reaction to employees campaigning against their companies, Ron Williams, the former CEO of insurance giant Aetna, said to *Quartz*, "I can't imagine that happening twenty years ago."[26]

Companies know that employees have more choices, and that they expect to live their values at work. As the *Los Angeles Times* reports, Google spent years "exhorting [employees] to 'bring their whole selves to work,'" and opening themselves up to this kind of activism ended up being the result.[27]

I was surprised when I spoke to Google managers about why they decided to issue a sustainability bond of $5.75 billion in 2020.

These kinds of bonds guarantee that the proceeds are used specifically for environmental and social purposes, such as lowering energy use and creating affordable housing. The issuance of the bond was particularly strange for a company like Google, which did not need the cash. I thought they would say that their reason for issuing it was that they could get a better deal that way, lowering the cost of financing. Instead, they explained that they did it for their employees, who care so much about sustainability issues that the company felt compelled to show its commitment in a public way, regardless of whether the company truly needed the money.

On the consumer side, the stories are not so different. The 2017 #DeleteUber movement is a prime example. Hundreds of thousands of riders quit using Uber after the company was accused of profiteering during a taxi strike in the wake of President Trump's international travel ban from a set of countries he linked to terrorism in 2017.[28] More customers left the app after sexual harassment scandals became known, particularly when former Uber employee Susan Fowler wrote an open letter about the company's culture of harassment and sexism, and CEO Travis Kalanick ultimately resigned from the company amid scandals of his own.

The media outlet Vox has written about consumer activism and how "conscious consumerism mean[s] more people are buying from brands they agree with and boycotting ones they don't."[29] Although young people are leading this activism (according to one study, the top factor determining where millennials decide to shop is a brand's reputation, with "32 percent more likely to prefer companies that reduce energy use, 30 percent more likely to prefer ones that donate to charity, 22 percent more likely to prefer ones that reduce packaging and 20 percent more likely to prefer companies that listen to the public"[30]), it is by no means limited to them. Vox cites Lawrence Glickman, a historian at Cornell University, who writes that two-thirds of consumers take part in at least one boycott each year.[31]

VALUE SHIFT:
FROM PHYSICAL CAPITAL TO HUMAN RELATIONSHIPS

The final element to discuss is the idea that people (and their opinions of your company) matter much more in the capital markets than they did in the past. The value of a business used to be driven largely by physical capital and manufacturing capacity: a successful business was one that could most effectively produce and distribute the objects it was selling, with the best machines and the largest factories. Now, success is driven by people—the quality of your employees and the relationships you have with your customers.

Companies can't afford to ignore the human factors in the way they could when people had fewer choices, less information, and no realistic way to demonstrate disapproval. Power has shifted, and the business world reflects this shift. What is driving the economy now isn't tangible assets but the intangible ones: the talents and skills within an organization, and the social capital developed outside of it. If you look at the most successful companies in the world—Google and Facebook, for example—they are dominated by human capital and understand that they need to preserve it. This is why Google and Facebook responded to activist employees by making changes, or at least promising to change. That is why Walmart announced, after consumer protests, that it would stop selling ammunition.[32]

If you look at market value (the total value of a company's shares in the market) relative to book value (the total value of all assets if liquidated), traditionally most of the market value of a company reflected its book value: the physical property, the machinery, the inventory. Eighty percent of the market value could be tied to these kinds of physical assets. Now, the percentage is reversed. Twenty percent of market value is tied to book value, and the other 80 percent is about intangible assets, the human and social capital developed over time (see figure 2.2). Google is a

trillion-dollar organization because of the social capital it has created, the human capital, the employees, the dedicated users, and
the intellectual property it has developed—not the servers running
the network and the campuses where the employees work.

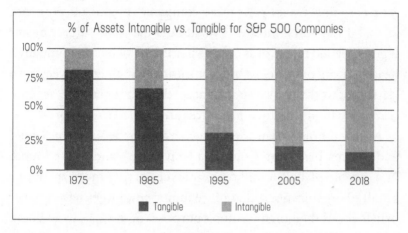

FIGURE 2.2

This switch over time has put employees and customers in the
driver's seat. It has given them the ability to have a stronger voice
and more influence, to live their values and preferences, and to
exert real power in the quest for purpose. It all adds up to a situation in which companies have to act differently and become more
aligned with the social and environmental concerns of the citizens
they seek to employ and serve. As it turns out, this is not a bad
thing for business. In fact, as the data below shows, purpose-driven
efforts pay off—at least if approached in the right way.

PURPOSE: A TRUE DIFFERENTIATOR

Having purpose as an organization, in the end, is good for business, but having purpose isn't satisfied by a senior leader making
a powerful speech, or a mission statement on a website. It's not

about what some have called "purpose-washing," using *purpose* as a buzzword but not actually having that purpose infuse the entire organization, the incentives, the compensation structures, the hiring process, the customer experience, and more. "Purpose is difficult to get right," says Carol Cone, reporting for *Fast Company*, "and easy to get wrong. As more companies pursue purpose, not all will do so authentically."[33] What does *authentic purpose* mean? It goes beyond nice words on a poster in the lobby at a company's headquarters or on its website. It means that all employees have clarity about the company's purpose, they feel agency to act consistently with it, and their incentives are aligned to support it.

My coauthors—Claudine Gartenberg from the Wharton School and Andrea Prat from Columbia University—and I have found, in a sample of half a million employees across more than four hundred organizations, that more junior employees have weaker beliefs about their organization's purpose (figure 2.3). In addition, when employees find a strong sense of meaning and purpose at work, and there is strong clarity about that purpose from senior management—communicated clearly, aligned with action, and diffused down into middle management—organizations perform better (figure 2.4).[34]

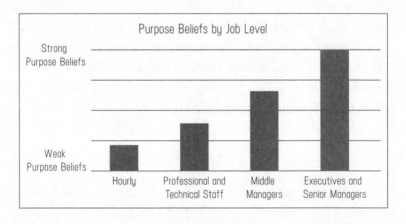

FIGURE 2.3

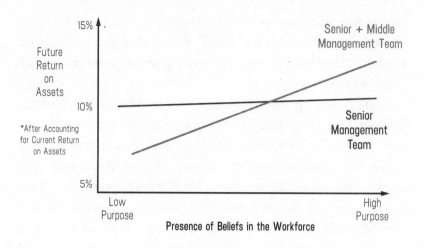

FIGURE 2.4

Our research proves the importance of the middle management layer. It is where strategy and vision meet execution. Senior managers can talk about hiring a diverse pool of candidates, and then developing their careers over time, but if nothing is actually put in place at the middle levels to carry these ideas through, the effort fails. The same is true if a consumer goods company talks about providing healthier products, but then doesn't put the right financial incentives in place to get the middle managers to develop and market these products. If they are still being evaluated based on quarterly earnings targets, not getting the budget to produce innovations to reformulate products or marketing dollars to convey new messages to customers, then there is no legitimate chance of the initiative finding success.

These are not trivial effects. Firms in which middle managers felt high purpose (giving high scores to statements like "my work has special meaning: this is not just a job," "I feel good about the ways we contribute to the community," "when I look at what we accomplish, I feel a sense of pride," and "I'm proud to tell others I work here") and high clarity (with high scores on statements like "management has a clear view of where the organization is going and how to get there") had higher future accounting and stock market performance—roughly a 6 to 7 percent premium in stock price per year.[35]

It is interesting that my research with Claudine Gartenberg, drawing on a sample of 1.5 million employees across more than one thousand publicly listed and privately held organizations, shows that corporate purpose can vary significantly depending on a company's ownership structure. Employees of public firms have a lower sense of purpose than those working for private firms.[36] Ben Chestnut, the cofounder of Mailchimp, an email marketing service, explains this effect: "I build things and get to watch customers buy and use them—that's tremendously satisfying. Sometimes I see companies build things I know are for investors—and what is the investor's purpose? Just to increase wealth. That doesn't align with my mission."[37] (Mailchimp has remained a private company since its founding in 2001.) Our research shows that commitment like this is a huge driver of purpose. Firms whose owners have a long-term ownership horizon, rather than those who have only been in place for a short time, are more likely to develop a stronger sense of purpose.[38]

Further research from Vanessa Burbano at Columbia University demonstrates a positive relationship between corporate social performance and attractiveness as an employer: firms with higher social performance ratings attract more applicants and can hire them for less money—and they will work harder.[39] The effects were strongest for the employees most critical to success. High-performing workers were more responsive to a social mission program than lower-performing workers and were willing to give up wages to work in a firm with that type of program.

Of course, finding the right talent for your organization requires real effort. A strong recruitment process that emphasizes people who prioritize personal mastery of their craft and who show deep passion for the purpose of the organization is important. My observation through the years has been that organizations that successfully attract high-performing, purpose-driven employees tend to invest greater-than-average resources into both the recruiting and onboarding processes. Companies need to show their commitment to finding great talent with actions, not just words.

In all, the research is quite clear: purpose matters, for both recruitment and performance. For this generation of employees and consumers—the "Impact Generation"—profits are won or lost based in part on how a company acts in the world, and whether the company allows people to live their values.

We talked about transparency earlier as one element of how employees and consumers can figure out how a company is behaving, but the topic deserves a larger discussion, especially in the context of how businesses are much less able to hide scandal in the age of social media than they were just a generation ago. In the next chapter, we will talk about how a big part of the new alignment is the lack of secrets, and how scandals are becoming known, making it impossible for companies to thrive unless they take a close look at their behavior in the world. We will also look at the metrics emerging to allow these behaviors to be announced to investors and the public.

Chapter Three

TRANSPARENCY AND ACCOUNTABILITY: NO MORE SECRETS

If you search Twitter for "corporate scandal" on any given day, something is bound to pop up. On the morning I wrote this, my search revealed an article about two leading automakers who, fifty years ago, knew that carbon emissions from their vehicles were contributing to climate change. Other headlines were about an Australian construction company's billion-dollar bribery scandal and a German electronic payments start-up that admitted to inventing two billion Euros that didn't exist as part of nearly a decade-long accounting fraud. If I'd continued to search, I'm sure I would have found even more. What might have gone unnoticed, unreported, and certainly unpublicized a generation ago is now just a click away. Something happens in a distant land, and all it takes is someone snapping a photo with his iPhone, writing a few lines on Facebook, sneaking a video, and it goes viral. Newspapers pick it up, and the story travels around the world before you know it. If I know something that enough people might care about, I have many ways, at no cost, in no time, with no real obstacles, to get it out there.

When I think of the rise of information about what companies are doing, I remember a conversation I had with Allen White, the cofounder of the Global Reporting Initiative. GRI has spent almost twenty-five years developing sustainability reporting standards and propagating them throughout the world, helping companies disclose their impacts on society, creating a common language around sustainability goals, and striving for global corporate transparency.

White started GRI in the wake of the *Exxon Valdez* oil spill, wanting to encourage more accountability, first around environmental issues and then expanding to social, governance, and economic issues. His vision was around giving all of us a greater voice when it comes to how companies behave. Shareholders and investors have always had a voice and the ability to get financial information about the companies they invest in, thanks to financial accounting standards. The rest of us on the outside did not have the data to know what companies were doing, and no real window into their behavior. Therefore, we couldn't have a voice; we couldn't express a preference for companies that acted one way over companies that acted in a different way, because we simply didn't know. If you don't have information, you can't make informed choices, and your freedom to express yourself in this way is limited.

The world today is different. In the 1990s, there was much press about the Nike sweatshop scandal. Suddenly people started paying attention to factory conditions. What they saw appalled them. We remember the Nike scandal so well because, for a long time, it was the only one out there that reached the public. Now, every time we open a newspaper, we see equivalents and worse. I'll talk in this chapter about the explosion of information and what we must do to make that information meaningful. I'll discuss metrics, benchmarks, and ultimately how these new measurements are redefining what success means for companies and how they have contributed to the virtuous cycle where the more we know, the more we care, and the more that good behavior makes a positive impact on corporate performance.

WHEN WORD GETS OUT: THE FALL OF FOXCONN

In my classes, I teach about Foxconn, the Chinese electronics factory, which supplies parts for Apple, Hewlett-Packard, and others. In the span of a few months in 2010, more than a dozen Foxconn workers committed suicide.

Conditions at the company were grim. Foxconn forbade conversations between employees, limited bathroom breaks to ten minutes every two hours, and often made employees work double or triple the legally permitted number of hours. However, for these young (the average age was twenty-one, and some workers were just fifteen years old), uneducated, low-skilled workers, often migrants from more rural parts of China, the jobs were highly desirable, considering the alternatives. Unlike some other, smaller manufacturers, Foxconn actually paid the workers what they were promised, gave them subsidies for housing and meals, and allowed them to choose to live for free in company dorms (a mixed blessing, as you'll see below).

Conditions had been getting worse for several years before the company entered the public's consciousness. There were at least two suicides in both 2007 and 2009. One occurred after a worker was suspected of losing an iPhone 4G prototype. UK journalists exposed subpar dormitory conditions in 2006, highlighting the lack of air-conditioning during the hot summer, which led to unpleasant odors, and workers referred to company housing as "the garbage dorm."[1]

Nevertheless, it took until the string of suicides in 2010 for the story to spread around the world. The suicide of nineteen-year-old Ma Xiangqian that January sparked particular media attention when Ma's sisters insisted that he had been beaten to death (there was evidence of scars and wounds on his body), and there were reports, which the company refuted, that Ma had damaged equipment and been assigned to clean toilets as punishment. As more and more suicides followed in short order, media coverage increased, and Apple sent Tim Cook, then its COO, to China along with two suicide prevention experts to investigate. In the end, Foxconn asked its employees to sign a "no suicide" pledge and installed netting around its building to catch jumpers. Its stock price dropped by 24 percent in 2010, and as of this writing sits at less than a quarter of what it was worth at its peak in 2007.

The rise of social media and the widespread diffusion of information now allow for companies like Apple to use machine-learning technologies to pick up potential problems in their supply chain before they rise to the level of tragedy that took place at Foxconn. These kinds of technologies can help companies avoid similar reputational disasters in the future.

INFORMATION ALONE IS NOT ENOUGH

A decade later, it is not just one-off reports about companies like Foxconn that make the headlines. With the increasing range of information sources, we do not need to rely only on media headlines; we now have data. Thousands of companies are now reporting environmental, social, and governance (ESG) information. Beyond the companies' own reports, researchers are systematically collecting data that go beyond the financial numbers and traditional metrics.

In chapter four, I discuss in detail a study about companies' responses to the COVID-19 pandemic. In this study, my colleagues and I relied on sentiment scores, using natural language processing data applied to thousands of news sources around the world, in eleven languages, to determine whether media coverage about particular companies was positive or negative. Negative scores, for example, typically applied to news about layoffs or the absence of paid sick leave, while articles about keeping workers safe during the pandemic tended to receive positive coverage and thus positive sentiment scores.

This study is just one example of new data collection technologies. Our ability to process information that would have been almost impossible to collect manually at scale not only expands the pool of possible data out there, but also gives us insights about how companies are behaving. That said, information—whether financial, anecdotal, or a sentiment score—can only get you so far. Our capacity to generate information is useful only to the extent that we can glean meaning from that data. If I tell you, for instance, that I have twenty-five billion red blood cells in my body, how can you interpret that information without benchmarks or standards? Does a typical person have more or fewer? Does it matter? Is it meaningful? Twenty-five billion red blood cells sounds like a lot, until I tell you that the average adult human has twenty-five *trillion* red blood cells, and to have one-thousandth of the average is a tremendously meaningful difference.

REPORTING AND TRANSPARENCY

For a long time, we didn't study what companies were doing when it came to their environmental or social impact. In fact, for a long time, we barely knew what was happening from the financial side. Financial reporting in the United States wasn't formulated until the early part of the twentieth century, and wasn't mandatory until the middle of the century. What we now take for granted—information about sales, assets, and other financial figures—was not made public by even the largest corporations back then. When it was suggested that accounting standards should be created to compare companies' financial performance, many commentators pushed back, reasoning that it is impossible to create methodologies to compute revenues or assets for all firms, and that such transparency would bring an end to the competitiveness of many companies. They were proven wrong. In fact, companies and capital markets have prospered because of the creation of financial accountability mechanisms, not despite them.

Standard reporting has matured over the past century from being merely a balance sheet, an income statement, and a cash flow report to far more, including discussion and analysis, explanatory material, and information about future goals. Still, for many people, this has not been enough, especially since companies now have a great degree of flexibility and discretion when it comes to their accounting principles and in deciding what material is included in their reports and what is omitted.

The idea of reporting around environment, social, and governance factors initially met with similar skepticism. While some thought that transparency would increase good behavior by corporations, others (including the head of the International Accounting Standards Board) believed that sustainability reporting would result in the same thing that happened once executive pay began to become public: occasional headlines, but no meaningful change.

The tide began to turn in the wake of high-profile disasters like the 1984 Union Carbide gas leak in India (commonly known as the Bhopal disaster) and the 1989 *Exxon Valdez* oil spill in Alaska. Blame for these tragedies fell, at least in part, on the idea that management had ignored health and safety issues. In 1995, when Royal Dutch Shell was criticized for alleged human rights violations, the company tried to repair the damage by becoming one of the first large corporations to publish a corporate social responsibility report, which they did for the first time in 1998. While others followed, without real standards there was huge potential for what is known as "goodwashing," when a company chooses what impacts to report, handpicking only the most favorable data.

Indeed, when thinking about whether transparency yields better behavior, it is hard to draw cause-and-effect conclusions. Companies that behave badly are less likely to disclose, and even companies that do voluntarily disclose may only tell their version of the story. We need comparability and benchmarking: Is the data being reported in a way that makes sense, that allows for comparisons between companies, and that gives us insight into whether the behavior is particularly meaningful, and particularly good or bad?

In our research, we have explored two threads regarding these topics. One is *accountability*—does having information lead to better behavior? The other is *value relevance*—can knowing how companies are performing on environmental, social, and governance metrics give us information that is useful going forward, that adds to what we understand about a company when merely looking at financial metrics? We can look at these issues one at a time.

ACCOUNTABILITY: VOLUNTARY VS. MANDATORY

Frequent watchers of the local news in any large metropolitan area are sure to see the occasional story about restaurant hygiene gone wrong, rats caught on camera in the windows of fast-food establishments, taking over after darkness falls. In 2010, New York City launched a restaurant letter-grading program. Eating establishments had to post in their windows a letter grade (A, B, or C) indicating their latest health inspection score.[2] The program provides a great example of mandatory data disclosure. Establishments couldn't choose to avoid it—no goodwashing possible, which means we can ask the question, can disclosure alone improve outcomes?

In this case, it did. Comparing the three years before the mandatory posting of letter grades to the three years afterward, there was a 35 percent increase in A-rated inspections (and a 5.3 percent per year decrease in salmonella poisoning citywide[3]). Another study showed that energy consumption decreased when customers were sent information comparing their energy usage to that of their neighbors.

On the other hand, health care report cards haven't had a significant effect on patient choices. Required disclosure of toxic emissions has not led to significant action. Merely having information can improve performance, but it doesn't always, and the ability to change behavior at a low cost is critical for these types of efforts to make a difference. Cleaning up a restaurant kitchen isn't a trivial issue, but it's manageable when the restaurant is faced with the alternative: a low rating plastered on the front window, causing customers to turn away. Changing an entire manufacturing process to lower emissions is a much larger endeavor, which may be why those efforts need more than just mandatory disclosure to motivate change.

Over the past decade, many countries have started to mandate various types of ESG reporting. In our research, my colleagues and I found that by following these mandates, disclosure and transparency have increased, and some companies have improved their performance on these ESG issues. Our research also found that, at the time these disclosure regulations were promulgated, the stock prices of the companies that weren't already disclosing the mandated information actually declined, even before any information was disclosed. That is because investors expect that companies with good news are already sharing it, and those not already sharing the information must have something to hide. Thus, the mandates do exactly what they are intended to do, leading to no more secrets.

VALUE RELEVANCE: IT'S A QUESTION OF MEANINGFULNESS

The more complicated hypothesis propagated by researchers in the early days of ESG reporting was whether transparency might not only lead to better performance as a result of accountability, but may also provide information that could improve predictions about future financial performance. In other words, was financial information actually a lagging indicator, and might it be the case that companies that did better on certain sustainability metrics were positioned to perform better in the future—not just in terms of sustainability but in terms of overall financial performance?

With this question in mind, Jean Rogers founded the Sustainability Accounting Standards Board in 2012. SASB seeks to develop and disseminate industry-specific sustainability standards, believing that the kinds of sustainability-related actions that are relevant to financial performance, or material, in one industry aren't necessarily material in every industry. For example, data privacy issues continue to increase in importance for commercial banks with the digitization of documentation and customer service. Their revenue growth is affected by customer trust, and their costs are also impacted by new regulatory burdens and potential legal disputes. In the case of agricultural companies, water management is emerging as a key issue given the droughts and risk of water scarcity exacerbated by climate change, thus affecting these companies' ability to produce and sell their products. Figure 3.1 on page 52 shows some of these differences between industries.

Guided by the SEC's definition of materiality, as defined by the United States Supreme Court—"presenting a substantial likelihood that the disclosure of the omitted fact would have been viewed by the reasonable investor as having significantly altered the total mix of information made available"—Jean hoped to create a framework for deciding what sustainability metrics each individual company ought to disclose to investors.[4]

When Jean and I first talked about her idea for SASB in early 2011, I thought it was a tremendous idea. Creating these industry standards could reduce goodwashing, increase comparability, and show investors around the world that there were certain pieces of material information that they were missing out on and ought to be demanding from companies. We were confident that investors were the ones with real leverage in this process. If they were actually insisting on disclosure, then companies would have no choice but to comply, for fear of not getting the capital they needed.

SASB has been a game changer, a wild success. I was on the Standards Council of SASB helping to create standards from 2012 to 2014. It made me realize how much resistance there was to changing the status quo. Regulators were doing little to help Jean and SASB. Corporate executives were very skeptical that investors would actually care. As it turned out, once we had these standards, people did care. Hundreds of companies agreed to adopt our standards, including huge ones like General Motors and JetBlue, and suddenly an increasing number of investors were demanding these disclosures from everyone. Once the standards existed, suddenly we had something meaningful, a way to compare companies to one another. There could be no more excuses about how sustainability was subjective, immeasurable, or immaterial.

POSITIVE IMPACT OF ESG FACTORS ON FINANCIAL PERFORMANCE

By the time SASB came along, many people had tried to determine the impact of ESG factors and whether doing good was actually translating to doing well. It was not until we understood that different industries might have different material factors that we could really figure out what to measure. Once we separated these factors and looked at whether performance on material ESG factors specifically made a difference in future financial performance, we found amazing results. Improvement on material measures of environmental, social, and governance performance was significantly predictive of future financial performance.

In a sample of more than twenty-three hundred companies, firms that were improving their performance on material ESG issues—those that were relevant for the industries they were in—did well, outperforming competitors by more than 3 percent annually, a hugely significant number. What was equally important was our finding that firms improving their performance on ESG issues that were not material in their industry exhibited little performance differential from their competitors, suggesting that companies need to deeply understand which ESG issues affect their competitiveness and how to focus their attention in productive ways.

It is indeed the case that different industries have very different sets of material issues. As illustrated in figure 3.1, you can see SASB's Materiality Map for the financial industry as compared to agricultural products companies. Commercial banks need to focus on issues like customer data privacy, access to finance for underserved populations, incorporation of environmental risks in loan provision, and strong anti-corruption practices to avoid money laundering and market manipulation, but there is little evidence of the materiality of these same issues for agricultural products companies. Instead, those companies have to consider their directly-produced greenhouse gas emissions, water management, the physical safety of employees, and crop-related risks and opportunities emerging from climate change. Focusing on what has been shown to matter in your business can make a real difference between ESG efforts that bear fruit and those that have little impact.[5]

In 2013, Bob Eccles from Oxford University and I wrote a provocative article titled "Sustainability in Financial Services Is Not About Being Green." By that, we did not mean that banks should not care about the environment. Rather, we were frustrated by the focus of many banks on reducing carbon emissions from their buildings and improving energy efficiency by switching from traditional incandescent light bulbs. While commendable, the impact of these efforts is immaterial to these businesses and frankly to the world. It would be far more important to focus on the environmental impact of the decisions they make around their financing

Dimension	General Issue Category	Commercial Banks	Agricultural Products
Environment	GHG Emissions		■
	Air Quality		
	Energy Management		■
	Water & Wastewater Management		■
	Waste & Hazardous Materials Management		
	Ecological Impacts		
Social Capital	Human Rights & Community Relations		
	Customer Privacy		
	Data Security	■	
	Access & Affordability	■	
	Product Quality & Safety		■
	Customer Welfare		
	Selling Practices & Product Labeling		
Human Capital	Labor Practices		
	Employee Health & Safety		
	Employee Engagement, Diversity & Inclusion		
Business Model & Innovation	Product Design & Lifecycle Management	■	
	Business Model Resilience		
	Supply Chain Management		■
	Materials Sourcing & Efficiency		■
	Physical Impacts of Climate Change		
Leadership & Governance	Business Ethics	■	
	Competitive Behavior		
	Management of the Legal & Regulatory Environments		
	Critical Incident Risk Management		
	Systemic Risk Management	■	

FIGURE 3.1

activities, the loans that they provide, and the risk management they do in order to avoid the next financial crisis.

Before our findings, researchers had been probing to find the relationship between ESG and financial performance for more than forty years, with conflicting results. There were more than 120 research papers published on the topic between 1972 and 1997, with no consensus. One study I conducted with Bob and Ioannis Ioannou from London Business School, analyzing 180 organizations, showed that companies identified as early ESG adopters in the 1990s outperformed competitors over the following fifteen years, but it was unclear whether we could generalize those results to broader samples and show which investments were likely to create value.

In an attempt to unpack this, we did further research. Using the SASB standards to guide the work made the direction of the relationship very clear. Doing these things matters now if you want to succeed in the future. Soon after we released our results, Credit Suisse reported similar outcomes, as did Russell Investments. Asset managers such as Rockefeller Capital Management found similar effects in their portfolios too.

In another study, with Jody Grewal from the University of Toronto and Clarissa Hauptmann of Oxford University, using a sample of thirteen hundred companies, we were able to show that disclosure of information on material ESG issues helped firms differentiate themselves from competitors, allowing investors to understand a company's unique competitive positioning.[6]

The research moved people in a way that the subjective case— "of course you should care about treating workers well, preserving the environment, promoting diversity, acting ethically, and more"—was never able to do. The new analytics of doing good had finally emerged. The SASB standards, and the data that flowed from them, overcame the resistance of corporate executives to engaging in discussions about what they were doing for the greater good of society and the world. Investors were now forcing answers because they knew it was ultimately going to affect their returns.

The effects showed up in every corner of the business world. I had a conversation with the CFO of a large chemical company not all that long ago—2019, in fact. He said that even two years earlier, no one during his investor road show asked any ESG-related questions. Now, he told me, at least 50 percent of the questions concerned these very issues. He had no choice but to care. The move from transparency to metrics to benchmarking to comparability to materiality had ultimately mobilized people to change their decision-making processes. This kind of virtuous cycle is causing a race to the top, and incentivizing companies to innovate more and more.

IMPACTING THE FUTURE: THE NEXT STEP

I teach my students about Solvay, a Belgian chemical company that developed a sustainable portfolio management tool back in 2008, in an attempt to determine the environmental impact of every product application. Executives wanted to make better-informed choices for the business. The effort resulted in Solvay becoming one of the first companies to combine sustainable management with financial decision-making. Seeing its environmentally favorable product applications outperform the environmentally harmful ones in terms of sales growth crystallized for CEO Ilham Kadri the value of this tool for driving the company's direction. Armed with this kind of data, Solvay decided in 2020 to move their efforts to the next level, launching a "One Planet" holistic approach to sustainability, and taking the lead in their industry to minimize resource consumption, reduce greenhouse gas emissions, and become a zero-waste company.

As Kadri told my Harvard Business School class in the spring of 2021, she saw sustainability as a way to differentiate the company and increase its price/earnings multiple. The company had historically underperformed, but a wholehearted commitment to sustainability could be a growth strategy that would unleash the full potential of the work they were doing. Sustainability wasn't just going to be a side project. It would in fact be fully integrated into everything the business did. Just a year into the One Planet approach, the strategy was already paying off. Solvay had launched partnerships to improve energy efficiency in tires sold by Michelin, and to recycle end-of-life electric battery metals with car manufacturer Renault and water, waste, and energy company Veolia to help move the world toward a more efficient and circular economy.

This full integration—sustainability as core to what a company does, and core to what we measure them doing—is the idea behind the impact-weighted accounts movement that I lead at Harvard Business School. The impetus to drive this effort comes from the same impulse that led me to participate with the Standards Council at SASB. I didn't want to be on the sidelines of this movement. I wanted to help create the change I wanted to see in the world. The Impact-Weighted Accounts Initiative is the next step forward for accountability reporting, and is making great progress toward impact transparency in the corporate world in just a few short years since its launch.

The project began in late 2018, when after a conference I met Sir Ronald Cohen, one of the foremost pioneers in venture capital and impact investing. We both felt that there were many metrics out there, and many companies doing amazing reporting, but still not enough. We felt that without true impact transparency we would never reach a point where companies could put impact at the heart of decision-making, right alongside risk and return. After speaking for about an hour, I realized how challenging and difficult the journey would be. Sir Ronald, in what I discovered to be his usual fashion, was undeterred. He turned to me and said, "George, let's do this."

As I said in chapter one, if I ask my students, "What is success in business?" more and more, the answer is not just today's profit. The impact-weighted accounts movement insists that we need to redefine as a society what success means, and in fact what profit means. We need to make sure that when we talk about a company's net profits, we are reflecting not just the money a company takes in, but the value it contributes to the world, or takes from it.

Impact-weighted accounting does just this. It puts everything a company does into monetary terms, and lets us calculate a company's earnings after taking into account its environmental impact, its customer impact, its employee impact, and so on. It provides tools to convert nonfinancial metrics into financial ones, in order to make sure that financial statements identify truly profitable companies. Just as we are not likely to celebrate an athlete known to be using illegal substances, we should not be celebrating companies that are profitable because they pollute, pay people at levels below a living wage, and sell addictive products that damage the health of their own customers. The real business leaders are the ones who create profits and generate positive impact at the same time, something that can absolutely be detected and calculated through a firm's impact-weighted earnings-per-share.

The bottom line is that if the purpose of a company is just to maximize short-term profits, then looking at earnings and other core financial metrics to judge performance is fine. But it's not, and so by looking merely at financial metrics, we create heavily distorted incentives. We may say we don't want companies to maximize only their financial performance, but if we judge them just on that, then what can we expect?

IMPACT-WEIGHTED ACCOUNTING: A GAME CHANGER

As my analysis with Sir Ronald, now chair of the leadership council of IWAI, shows, 15 percent of companies with positive profits in 2018 would find them eliminated if environmental impacts were taken into account. Looking specifically at airlines, accounting for the environmental costs of Lufthansa—$2.3 billion—and American Airlines—$4.8 billion—would make both companies unprofitable. For the airline industry, for paper and forest products, electric utilities, construction materials, containers and packaging, almost all companies would see at least 25 percent of their profits eliminated.

Not all results are negative. Some companies create enormous positive impact through their employment practices and their products. To illustrate the power of the analysis, let's look at the employment impact of Apple and Facebook, the environmental impact of two leading tire producers, and the product impact of two airlines (see figure 3.2). You can see that there are significant differences between companies in the same industry, sometimes (as in the airline example) moving in opposite directions.

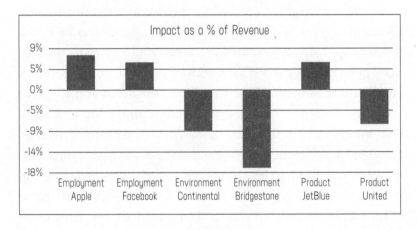

FIGURE 3.2

Not every company sees its numbers affected in the same way, which is, ultimately, the point. There is a stark difference between companies when analyzed in this way, and it is the ones who see their numbers rise most when true impact is reflected that we should be highlighting, celebrating, and trying to replicate. Intel, as one example, created approximately $4.5 billion of positive impact by providing high-wage jobs and benefits such as childcare support and paid sick leave, including in areas of high unemployment. That number would be even greater if Intel had a truly diverse workforce that represented the demographics of the population and if senior management was as diverse as at lower levels. By seeing these numbers in black and white, and understanding the levers that could be adjusted to change them for better or worse, companies can actually judge the impact of their decision-making. If a company is on the fence about whether to expend added efforts to address worker conditions in its factories, for instance, it can use impact-weighted accounting to get an idea of how much value they might ultimately create as a result of that change.

Armed with a metric, we can think big. Imagine governments using impact-weighted accounting metrics to tax companies for the harm they do, or provide direct economic incentives for a positive impact. Impact-weighted accounting also gives us the ultimate point of comparison for investors, consumers, and potential employees to integrate these factors into the decisions they make about what companies to fund, to buy from, and to work for. Right now, analysis shows that there is already a significant correlation between environmental damage and lower stock market valuations in a number of industries. Where we do not yet see the same correlation may not be because of a lack of materiality, but because of the lack of a way to measure it. Transparency—especially in the easy-to-analyze form that impact-weighted accounting provides— is the key to making more and more sustainability factors material in more and more industries. Impact-weighted accounting can ultimately be a game changer in aligning society and business, the master analytic to drive doing good.

Efforts such as IWAI enable the democratization of sophisticated tools for companies that may not have the resources to develop them on their own, as Solvay has. Creating open-access methodologies, data, and tools will allow companies of any size to gain decision-driving insights about their impact on the world that they would otherwise not have been able to generate.

We are not there yet, though the truth is that when Sir Ronald and I began discussing impact-weighted accounting back in 2018, I had no idea it would catch on as quickly as it has. More than a hundred leading companies around the globe are now practicing some type of impact-weighted accounting, and the list keeps growing. One is Danone, the French food leader. It claims to be the first company in the world to adopt what it calls a "carbon-adjusted" earnings-per-share metric, to help investors understand the impact of the company's greenhouse gas emissions.[7] With this metric, Danone can show its profitability after accounting for the environmental damage it creates. The company announced in 2015 that it aims to become carbon neutral by 2050—and this is a step toward holding itself accountable for that goal. As a purpose-driven company—an "Entreprise à Mission" in France, and a certified B Corp—Danone is required to act in a way that benefits its customers' health as well as the planet.

Mathias Vicherat, general secretary of Danone, told CNBC that the new measure is also about recruiting great employees, along exactly the same lines as I discussed in chapter two. "[I]f you want to recruit the good talent," Vicherat said, "after business school, or after university, if you want to maintain the good employees inside the company, being a company with a good social impact is something that adds value from an HR point of view."[8] Employees, as the previous quote suggests, can be major forces in the push for impact transparency—and help create better business environments and societal outcomes at the same time.

THE NEXT STEPS: WHAT IS TO BE DONE?

The sooner governments mandate the publication of impact-weighted accounts, and require companies and investors to join in the effort to tackle climate change, inequality, and so forth, the better off our society will be. In the meantime, we each have a role to play:

- If you lead a company, you must start to measure and communicate your impact-weighted performance.
- If you are an employee, engage with senior leaders and ask for impact transparency from the company.
- If you are an investor, you need to demand impact transparency from the companies in which you invest, and use impact-weighted numbers to assess opportunities and risk.
- If you are a policymaker, you should be working to mandate the publication of impact-weighted accounts, and introducing taxes and incentives based on both profit and impact.
- Since we are all consumers, we should make an effort to buy the products of companies that deliver positive impact.

I truly believe that all of this will make a difference.

Impact transparency can actually reshape capitalism. By shifting the pursuit of profit away from creating problems to bringing solutions to the world, we can redefine success so that its measure is the positive impact—and not just the money—we make during our lifetimes.

In the next chapter, we start to see how the trends described in the first three chapters have come to fruition in the world. Companies, more and more, are taking on big roles in society that we would not have expected just a few years ago. They are providing public goods, and affecting the world in ways we aren't accustomed to seeing outside of government institutions. When those impacts are positive, we are seeing companies rewarded in tremendous

ways. When the impacts are negative, we are seeing more accountability than ever. Good behavior is becoming more beneficial, and
bad behavior is becoming more costly. Chapter four explains how
companies are behaving, and how the world is responding; when
we turn to chapter five, we will discover how businesses can use
these trends to their advantage.

Chapter Four

THE EVOLVING CONSEQUENCES OF CORPORATE BEHAVIOR

Corporations, by any measure, have grown larger and more influential over the past generation. During the 2010s, the world's top five hundred companies were responsible for half of the total market value of the more than fifty thousand publicly traded companies around the world. The Global 500 sold products and services worth more than $22 trillion, controlled assets valued at more than $100 trillion, and in any given year spent close to $1.5 trillion and $500 billion in capital and research and development expenditures, respectively. In every year of the past decade, Toyota alone spent more than $10 billion on research and development. Only sixteen countries have a greater R&D budget—and that's looking at just one company. Corporate influence, for better or worse, is extraordinary.

In 2015, I presented to an audience of executives the graph in figure 4.1, which shows the percentage of economic resources and outcomes for the five hundred largest publicly listed companies relative to all publicly listed companies globally. I was making the case that economic resources and outcomes were concentrated in a few very large companies and that their impact was spotlighted in new ways. While most of the people in the audience worked for Global 500 companies, they had never before realized the amount of economic concentration in the marketplace.

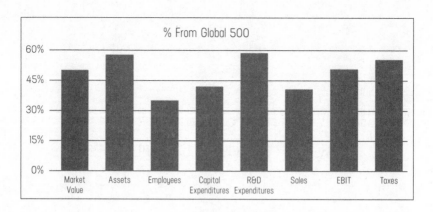

FIGURE 4.1

At the same time that this concentration grew, our biggest global problems—climate change, air pollution, tropical deforestation, water scarcity, declining biodiversity, and inequality, to name just a few—had become increasingly complex and required true global coordination. My argument was that business had increasingly gained power over other institutions. As a result, there was now a countervailing force where governments and civil society enforced higher accountability about the way companies affect society, making ESG issues financially material for companies. Their profitability, risk, and valuation had become a function of their ESG performance.

THE ROLE OF BUSINESS IN MEETING THE ESG CHALLENGE

From a logistical perspective, huge conglomerates operating around the world are often better positioned than governments to meet national and global challenges. When Hurricane Katrina hit Louisiana in August 2005, leading to more than twelve hundred deaths and $125 billion in damages, Walmart, not the federal government, emerged with one of the most impressive logistics operations in the world. The company was first to provide much-needed food and clothing to the affected residents. Why? Businesses are in many cases more agile, more innovative, and more capable than government bureaucracies. In other cases, businesses have been able to coordinate cross-border efforts, demonstrating greater freedom to work across city, state, and national boundaries than most government entities.

Many corporations now rival governments in size and scope. Assisted by globalization, the development of management science, and the growth of technology-enabled communications facilitating large-scale coordination, corporations have become quasi-governmental entities in some important ways. They can pursue programs to fight climate change, world hunger, and inequality, and often make real progress. Even without regulation forcing them to act in ways that go beyond revenue generation, cost cutting, and profit maximization, many companies take on these burdens eagerly and willingly.

For some, this is frightening, especially as we think about how much power a small number of for-profit institutions hold. For others, it's not scary at all; rather, they see it as a triumphant unleashing of the innovation capacity of the free market. Wherever you fall along this spectrum, it is undeniable that the enormous size of many companies has created a new set of expectations about the role those corporations should play in society.

In the wake of the COVID-19 pandemic, in the spring of 2020, US companies were criticized because only an estimated 58 percent of US service workers were entitled to paid sick leave according to one 2019 survey.[1] Yet, perhaps counterintuitively, we could argue that the fact that 58 percent of US service workers were entitled to paid sick leave is hugely positive in an environment where regulation largely did not require it. These companies—covering more than half of all workers—decided on their own to spend the money to give their employees a costly benefit not required by law. Of course, some of these companies were compelled to give benefits like these due to the forces of competition, but the fact that not all companies that directly compete against one another offer such benefits suggests that competition is only part of the story. Different management beliefs and strategies seem to play a role.

The fact that we see this as something to criticize rather than celebrate should tell us something about our expectations of companies in today's world. We largely believe that they ought to be good citizens and make efforts even without governmental requirements. We trust them, at least according to some surveys, more than we trust government. In fact, in one survey, 76 percent of people said that CEOs should be the ones to take the lead on change instead of waiting for governments to dictate progress.[2] Public trust in government, on the other hand, is at an all-time low. (In 1958, 73 percent of Americans trusted their government; by 2020, that number had fallen to just 20 percent.[3])

I do not mean to say we don't need governments, or that corporations can or should supplant them. Part of what governments can do is maintain the incentive structure that drives corporations to act for the public good. Businesses, both large ones (with their stupendous wealth and resources and their tremendous human capital) and smaller companies (with their own missions and resources) are now expected to step up to meet social goals. What is amazing is that they are largely doing so.

They do so because they can—they've grown large enough and influential enough that they have the ability to make an impact when it comes to the world's biggest and most complex problems—and they do so because they should, both from a moral perspective as well as from a strictly financial perspective. Companies that extend themselves in socially beneficial ways see a premium in the financial markets, and experience advantages across a number of other dimensions as well (recruiting talent, access to capital, investor appeal, and more). Companies that behave badly see consequences as well.

THE IMPACT OF TAKING ACTION

I talked in chapter one about Paul Polman and Unilever, but of course Polman, and now his successor, Alan Jope, are not the only leaders moved to take broad action toward sustainability. Daniel Servitje, the chairman and CEO of Grupo Bimbo, a global producer of baked goods (owner of the Entenmann's, Arnold Bread, and Sara Lee brands, among many others), headquartered in Mexico, has worked to improve the nutrition of his company's products as well as conserve water, reduce its carbon footprint, and improve working conditions. "Our sustainability program comes from our purpose as a business," Servitje has said. "To put some teeth to the ground, we asked ourselves, 'Who are the stakeholders we need to fulfill our purpose?' The answer was our associates, our consumers and society as a whole."[4]

These examples exist all around the world. Adrian Gore is the founder and chief executive of Discovery, a South Africa–based life, health, and auto insurance company that has a stated purpose of making people healthier. The company incentivizes customers to live better lives—25 percent off at grocery stores if they buy healthy food, rebates for going to the gym, trackers in cars that reward safe driving through discount premiums and gas purchases.[5] Employees at Discovery get bonuses for coming up with radical new ways to push subscribers toward healthier living. The data backs up the claims of reduced health care costs and longer life expectancy. Customers love saving money with the incentives. It's a great business model. Healthier customers mean fewer payouts and higher profits. In addition, employees love to work there because they feel like they are actually making a positive difference.

Even Walmart, often maligned, has turned itself around in past years. Beyond its efforts surrounding Hurricane Katrina, the company has made tremendous strides toward reducing its environmental footprint and tackling its impact on the workforce. This is important because the company is the largest US private-sector employer, with more than one million employees. When the company announced wage increases in 2015, its stock price initially tanked and CEO Doug McMillon was grilled on national television. He defended the move, explaining that it would benefit the company's long-term profitability by increasing employee productivity, lowering employee turnover, and improving customer satisfaction and loyalty.[6] At first, these arguments were ignored. Initially, expenses increased and profits declined as the firm invested more resources in its employees, but, in the end, the move worked. Walmart increased its sales growth and profitability, and joined Polman and Unilever on the sustainable side of the ledger.

Corporate efforts can even lead the way toward making a real impact on the global environment—not just minimizing the damage, but in fact engineering great benefit. Natura &Co is a Brazil-based personal care and cosmetics group that includes The Body Shop and Avon Products, and has been recognized for its innovation and exceptional performance over the past two decades. The company boasts that it uses Amazon forest ingredients sourced sustainably, but this isn't just marketing.[7] Fascinating research by Anita McGahan and Leandro Pongeluppe of the University of Toronto has shown that Natura's entry into specific municipalities in the Amazon rain forest helps to preserve forested areas.[8] Using satellite imaging, information on crop yields, and carbon density, the authors were able to tie Natura's stakeholder management strategy to the cultivation of forest-generated crops rather than clear-cutting leading to deforestation, a huge problem for the Amazon rain forest and for the world. In part because of these efforts, in 2019, the United Nations recognized Natura with its UN Global Climate Action Award, the most important climate change award in the world.

Taking real action to help the planet requires genuine effort, money, sacrifice, and prioritization. The difference between companies that take seriously the idea of acting with all of their stakeholders in mind and those who might not be willing to back up their words with actions becomes most stark during a crisis. This is exactly what we saw as COVID-19 emerged in early 2020.

MEETING THE CHALLENGE OF COVID-19

As I write this, the story of COVID-19 continues to unfold. Governments of course moved—some effectively, some less so—to meet the urgent needs the pandemic created, but the surprising part for many observers was that companies moved as well.

It is a stark change from a generation ago that people really did hope and expect that companies would respond productively when faced with a crisis like COVID-19—and were happy to criticize them if they did not. There was an almost-instantaneous focus on what companies were doing, across a wide range of measures. The results of these efforts are unclear right now, but we can look at the motivations, analyze the choices, and make some predictions as to what will come of these attempts to put sustainability ahead of short-term financial maximization in the setting of crisis.

It's important, though, to realize that to even examine this kind of corporate action was the result of increased transparency. There is not just increased sustainability reporting on a formal level, but because the public demands it, the media and other watchdog organizations now cover it. In addition, social media tools like Facebook and Twitter enable grassroots reporting of corporate activities—from employees, customers, and others in the know.

JUST Capital—the organization that named Microsoft its most JUST company three years running—was founded in 2013 as a registered charity to measure and rank companies on issues of sustainability and service to stakeholders. In the wake of the coronavirus crisis, the organization set up a tracker on its website that aggregated the responses of the hundred largest companies in the United States across fifteen dimensions, including offering bonuses or financial assistance to employees, community relief efforts, executive pay cuts, customer accommodations, paid sick leave, and work-from-home options.[9] I spoke at an event with Martin Whita-ker, the JUST Capital CEO, when he talked about how tracking the behavior of companies allows us to understand which companies truly value their stakeholders, especially when hard times hit.

Their findings during the pandemic ranged broadly, going from aerospace and defense company Northrop Grumman (85,000 US employees), where JUST Capital found no reports of any crisis-related efforts, to PepsiCo (114,000 US employees), which stepped up to offer a comprehensive plan, including backup dependent care to employees, paid sick leave, $45 million to a community relief fund, 50 million meals delivered to at-risk families around the world, new work-from-home policies, and more.

Nearly all of the hundred companies analyzed offered some-thing to a combination of employees, consumers, and the commu-nity to help during crisis conditions, even those businesses whose operations were relatively unaffected. Verizon promised that cus-tomers would have uninterrupted access to their internet and cable television even if they couldn't pay the bills.[10] LVMH (the French luxury goods conglomerate whose subsidiaries include Louis Vuit-ton, Givenchy, and Dior) converted its cosmetics production facili-ties to make hand sanitizer for distribution free of charge by French health authorities.[11] Zoom offered its videoconferencing products free to schools and educators to help with virtual learning efforts.[12]

We have already discussed the findings that purpose-driven companies with sustainability initiatives that tie directly to business functions ultimately outperform their competitors. That doesn't necessarily mean it is any easier for companies to make the leap and actually take action. First, it is very hard to know in advance what is going to turn out to be material to the core business—which initia-tives will pay dividends and which won't. Second, these activities are expensive, and increased financial performance will not always make up for the initial costs. Third, to spend money when you are hemorrhaging business in the wake of a crisis, when you do not know how you're going to make payroll, or how you're even managing to stay alive as a company, goes against perhaps every instinct of a business leader.

In April 2020, when we were still in the midst of crisis, my coauthors at State Street Associates (where I am an academic partner)— Stacie Wang, Alex Cheema-Fox, Bridget Realmuto LaPerla, and I released the first research paper looking at corporate resilience and response during the COVID-19 pandemic.[13] We analyzed a sample of 3,078 global companies with $59 trillion in market capitalization. To do this, we used big data from thousands of sources and performed sentiment analysis on company responses related to their employees, suppliers, and customers. We found that companies that responded by prioritizing the safety of their employees and suppliers and providing on-demand services to customers outperformed their peers by about 2.2 percent (see figure 4.2) in terms of stock returns during the thirty-two days of the sample (even after accounting for differences in industry membership or other firm characteristics across the two groups).

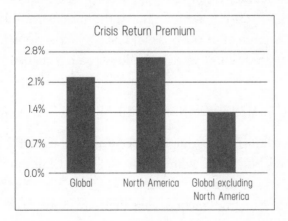

FIGURE 4.2

This is a significant finding. It shows that acting with an eye toward all of the company's stakeholders is beneficial. It also challenges the notion, advocated by several corporate executives, that investors put them in shackles and make them behave in a short-termist, "mind your business" kind of way. As I describe in chapter five, the root of the problem can often be traced back to the incentives and culture inside a company, not the investor attitudes surrounding it.

Yet, to look at the data and say that sustainability efforts lead to stronger financial performance, and therefore every company should do absolutely everything it possibly can, is missing the subtlety of the case. If it were that simple, and that obvious, we would not see companies like New York Sports Club decline to refund member dues in the face of the government telling people not to leave their homes,[14] or the shared workspace firm WeWork staying open during the pandemic and forcing its clients to pay their contracted fees.[15]

Short-term financial needs inevitably forced the hand of some companies, which could not afford to take hits during the pandemic. Other firms accepted the financial hits in the hope that in the long run their good behavior would lead to financial benefit. The overwhelming examples of good corporate citizenship during the COVID-19 crisis make it clear that the business world takes the growing alignment of purpose and profit very seriously. What is material to these companies in the long run has changed.

MISALIGNMENT, SCANDAL, AND THE ROLE OF LEADERS

I've been talking in this chapter largely about successful efforts to behave well, but, just as with New York Sports Club and WeWork, companies don't always behave in the most socially friendly ways. It may in fact seem from the news like there are more corporate scandals than ever, but I believe the reality is that far more behavior is considered scandalous, and, because of greater transparency, these scandals are now brought to light. The important question, in my view, is what happens when companies are hit by these scandals.

Few corporate scandals of recent years were bigger than the revelation in the summer of 2016 that employees of the retail banking unit of Wells Fargo had sold thousands of unnecessary banking products to customers, and opened more than a million unauthorized accounts. Ultimately, the company paid a huge price, nearly $3 billion between government fines and civil and criminal penalties. The company's market capitalization fell by $20 billion. Top leaders lost millions of dollars and were either terminated or forced to resign. The bank's 160-year-old reputation was destroyed.

In Brazil, while Natura was delivering meaningful positive impact through its efforts, the entire country was deeply impacted by the Petrobras oil scandal. A total of more than $5 billion in bribes and kickbacks changed hands as construction executives colluded to inflate project bids and grossly overcharge the company, paying Petrobras employees huge sums to enable the fraud and politicians to keep quiet and allow the scheme to perpetuate for years.[16]

Media reports were quick to blame a culture of corruption in Brazil. "Brazilians have a saying when the rich and powerful are arrested: 'It always ends with a pizza party . . .' meant to suggest that the justice system is rigged in favor of the elites," wrote the *New York Times*. "The accused are said to avoid prison and then celebrate by ordering pizza."[17] This time, that didn't happen. The CEO ended up sentenced to serve eleven years in prison.[18]

Activities once brushed aside or explained away as the inevitabilities of doing business (taking advantage of bank customers, for instance) are no longer acceptable. Gender-based discrimination, sexual harassment, mistreatment of factory workers, excess pollution and other environmental degradation, and many more problematic behaviors have risen to the level where they deeply damage a company and its employees. Bad behavior is costly and hard to avoid without genuine, wholesale, and companywide commitment to ESG principles.

For more than a decade, I've been studying scandals like the ones at Petrobras and Wells Fargo, and, most important, the environments that enable them. Accepting corruption means that fighting it is not a priority, and when it is not, bad things happen. It's not that (all) leaders at scandal-ridden firms encourage bad behavior. My research with my colleague Professor Paul Healy, using archival data on hundreds of organizations as well as field studies, found that many understand the importance of investing in systems that encourage compliance and they consistently demonstrate expectations that employees will act with integrity. However, they put outperforming competitors and impressing investors higher on the priority list than the enforcement of legal and ethical standards, and so those priorities end up being the primary drivers of workers' behavior.

In the service of profit, these leaders overlook shady business practices, and don't always punish employees found to be misbehaving. The rest of the organization notices, and behaves accordingly. The chair of a board of directors of an industrial company told me once that bad behavior had become so common that when he faced perpetrators of egregious behavior, their response was: "Everybody does that. I don't see anything wrong with it." Compliance becomes one more box to check rather than a critical part of the corporate culture.

Certainly the effects of being caught behaving badly, should that behavior become public, are clear: fines, reputational damage, stock price collapse. If you asked the executives at Wells Fargo if they wish they hadn't been caught fraudulently opening accounts, the answer would be unambiguously clear, but most people assume that if being caught wasn't an issue, morality aside, of course there would be economic benefits to ignoring the law. This isn't actually the case. The research Healy and I did led to an unexpected discovery: Business that emerges from illegal activity actually doesn't turn out to be worth the effort, even if you assume zero consequences for the behavior.

Siemens, the huge German multinational industrial manufacturing firm, found itself mired in a bribery scandal in 2004, eventually paying a $1.6 billion fine, the largest in modern corporate history at the time.[19] (Airbus now holds the unfortunate record, paying $4 billion in 2020.[20]) Audits conducted after the bribery scandal found that because the bribes were so substantial, they ate up all of the profits from the transactions. The result was similar when we studied a sample of 480 organizations whose sales growth was higher than their peers with better anti-corruption ratings, but profitability was lower. Indeed, we found that the sales growth that emerged from illegal deals was entirely offset by the reduced profits. Thus, there was no economic benefit (for the shareholders, at least; the individuals with their pay tied to geographic or divisional sales growth did get nice bonuses), and that's without considering the substantial risk of discovery and punishment. That risk of discovery—and the consequences for companies with poor anti-corruption ratings—is significant; those companies had a 28 percent higher chance of having a future scandal covered by the media.

BAD CORPORATE BEHAVIOR VS. ILLEGAL ACTS

It may strike you as inappropriate to compare the kinds of scandals I've talked about in this chapter—bribery, kickbacks, unambiguously criminal activities—with the kind of garden-variety indifference to social impact that I am arguing against throughout most of this book. There is a real difference, you might be thinking, between a company that doesn't care much about pollution or giving workers paid sick leave and a company that is literally breaking international law. Traditionally, that would be exactly the way to approach this analysis. If something was legal—polluting up to the edge of a regulatory limit, paying workers in ways that were entirely within their legal rights—a CEO would proudly stand up and defend the behavior, saying that profits come first, and anything the company can legally do to maximize those profits was fair game.

However, the line isn't quite so clear anymore. The differences between garden-variety "bad" corporate behavior and scandal-generating behavior are in fact disappearing. This is in part because more bad behavior is being discovered. Companies that suffered scandals involving, say, their supply chains were rarely noticed in a world before social media. Now, technology allows us to monitor and collect data on such incidences at massive scale.

RepRisk, a global ESG data science company, monitors supply chain labor issues and environmental violations for more than 165,000 companies around the world, providing information to investors and companies as they seek to protect their brands and reputations. But it is not just about being found out. It's about a change in the moral understanding of appropriate corporate conduct. Even decades ago, the most profit-focused CEO would usually admit that just because child labor was widespread somewhere along the supply chain, and likely would never be discovered, did not mean that it was okay. But child labor was the extreme case. Now, more issues are considered nearly as outrageous. Things like environmental pollution and gender discrimination are becoming societally unacceptable, just like child labor. Think about the #MeToo movement. Harassment, in the past, was often swept under the rug. Companies allowed executives to stay employed, and some even got promoted to the top, despite credible allegations against them and certainly in the face of rumors and bad reputations. Gender discrimination, poor treatment of low-wage workers, harm to the climate, and much more weren't making headlines, and they were sadly seen as within the norms of the business community. The Catholic Church for decades ignored allegations of child molestation, protecting clergy and keeping them from prosecution, until the world started to notice and care.

It doesn't take a situation like that at Petrobras to create a damaging scandal. Poor ESG performance—not prioritizing these issues, not taking a stand, not leading the way—is itself a scandal and can lead to huge repercussions.

BREAK FREE: TURN GOOD BEHAVIOR
INTO A COMPETITIVE ADVANTAGE

One of the lessons to be pulled from these experiences is that even if everyone in an industry is acting in a certain way, it does not mean that your company has to go along with it. You can lament how behaving well will put you at a disadvantage, or you can find a way to turn good behavior into a competitive advantage and use it to achieve breakthrough success. Occidental Petroleum is one company that illustrates this point. In November 2020, the company announced a goal of reducing greenhouse gas emissions to become net-zero by the year 2040.

For an oil company, this was an aggressive move, but CEO Vicki Hollub looked into the future and saw that the oil and gas business would have to change dramatically as the world becomes more concerned about climate change. She believed the company would ultimately be better positioned as a carbon management company than by selling oil. In other words, she wanted to change the definition of the business the company is in.

Occidental may or may not succeed in its efforts to pivot its business propositions to directives far less prone to future scandal and consequences, or it might all be marketing and PR—but it's a phenomenon worth noticing, one that I expect to see more of. Even cigarette manufacturer Philip Morris has committed to transform its business to contribute to a smoke-free world! As industries find themselves waylaid by bad press and harmed reputations, innovative companies will look for ways to separate themselves, to declare that they are different, and make concrete moves toward illustrating those differences.

WHY YOU SHOULD CARE

I am sometimes asked why I need to care about any of this if I am doing nothing wrong. Sure, organizations have problems, but if I am not the person leading the organization, and I'm not personally doing anything ethically corrupt, why do I need to worry about it? Many people, especially young people like my students, believe that as long as they do the right thing, they will be okay. They keep their eye on developing their own careers, on controlling the things within their sphere of influence, and figure that nothing above their level can affect them.

Research as well as anecdotal evidence prove this wrong. Not only the top people at Wells Fargo suffered post-scandal. Careers up and down the corporate hierarchy saw significant impacts; even people who did nothing wrong were tainted by association.

What happens to an organization has implications for everyone, even the people who have nothing to do with the problem situation. In a study I performed with my colleagues Boris Groysberg from Harvard Business School and Eric Lee from West Point, involving more than two thousand managers who had switched employers, we discovered that people coming from companies affected by scandals were paid almost 4 percent less than their peers.[21] That salary difference persisted over time. The more senior and closer in functional proximity a person is to the epicenter of the scandal (the marketing manager in a sales scandal or a financial manager in an accounting scandal), the bigger the effect.

As part of that project, I talked to a senior executive who had been at Lehman Brothers, an organization tainted by poor governance and risk management. He confirmed that senior managers were affected more severely than junior employees, who were not stigmatized. This executive wasn't involved in the part of the business that broke down. He had nothing to do with the financial crash, but it still became difficult for him to continue his career in the financial industry because he, nevertheless, was stigmatized by association. There were long-term repercussions for him, and he had a tremendous amount of trouble finding a new job.

So, what can people do? Before being caught up in a scandal, you need to take a hard look at the entire organization you are working for. You need to make sure you are acting as a steward for that organization and doing what you can to move it in the right ethical direction. At a minimum, you need to understand the law and the implicit norms of the industry, especially if you are working in a country you are unfamiliar with.

FUTURE OUTLOOK: STILL MORE PROGRESS TO BE MADE

Bad behavior has become more costly, and good behavior has proven to yield rewards—but the fact that scandals still regularly make the news tells us that our work is not done. We need only look at the varied responses to the COVID-19 pandemic as evidence. My prediction is that the companies who prove capable of looking past their own short-term interests will find that they are rewarded in the market in the end. Furthermore, the efforts they have pursued in crisis might give them a push toward new ways of thinking about problems that go far beyond the current pandemic, to climate change, employee welfare, and more. The next great breakthroughs may even emerge when times seem most bleak, because of employees everywhere in the value chain unleashing their ingenuity in discovering solutions to critical challenges.

So far, I have laid out an extraordinary new landscape of trends, data, and evidence that companies are behaving differently, and that society's expectations and desires concerning corporate behavior have changed. In the second half of the book, I will bring it all together. We will examine how you—as a leader, as an investor, and as an employee—can take advantage of the new alignment between purpose and profit. What do you do if you are running a company, deciding how to grow your money, or thinking about the course of your career?

In chapter five, we look at how a range of companies are figuring out how to make these trends work for them, and the tactics they are using to make themselves more sustainable. In chapter six, we look at how to build on those tactics and analyze the six broad categories of opportunity to create value in a world where sustainability matters for the bottom line. In chapter seven, we turn to investors, and the roles they play in maintaining the forces that are pushing companies to care about their behavior. Finally, in chapter eight, we look at how we can all approach these ideas as we examine our lives and our careers.

It is extraordinary how quickly the world has realized the relevance, importance, and potential impact of companies doing good while still working to make a profit. It is now up to all of us to understand how to put these ideas into play.

Part II

Execution:
How to Implement
Purpose-Driven
Initiatives

Chapter Five

THE TACTICAL PATH TO PROFITABLY DOING GOOD

I often speak to business leaders around the world about the kinds of trends covered in Part I. It used to be that I was met with much skepticism and doubt. Leaders insisted that while, say, using expensive solar energy would surely be great for the environment, like everything else it came at a cost, and pushing the envelope on sustainability issues would inevitably be bad for the bottom line. No one doubts that paying workers above-market wages, lowering carbon emissions, cleaning up factories, providing paid sick leave, improving product packaging, seeking organic certification, or almost any other ESG effort is worthwhile in a vacuum. Of course every well-intentioned business leader would do these things if they could. It's just that there are trade-offs, and for a business to survive, it can't spend money on everything, and be a perfect global citizen on all possible fronts.

This is the traditional view, and, indeed, ESG strategies that don't end up improving overall financial performance are still absolutely punished by the marketplace. Doing the right thing is not an all-access pass to breakthrough success. Nevertheless, companies have shown that you can do this and do it well, yielding positive results. We have already looked at some of these companies—Natura, Unilever, Oatly. Countless others exist, like Toyota, pioneering the development of hybrid vehicles and issuing itself an "environmental challenge" to reach zero carbon dioxide emissions and have a net positive environmental impact by 2050, or the pharmaceutical company Novo Nordisk working to reduce chronic diseases, eliminate its environmental impact, and move to 100 percent renewable power throughout its supply chain. These companies are finding success. How have they done it?

Starting now, we'll examine what business leaders can do to make alignment work for them. Make no mistake, this is not always easy; in fact, it is usually quite hard. Executing well can be costly for businesses, and personally costly for the individuals at the top of these businesses, because it requires long-term thinking, often short-term sacrifice, and taking risks. To move beyond measures that competitors will quickly imitate and find genuine competitive advantage through sustainability is an uncertain path—until one company leads the way and makes it all look easy.

If it were as simple as it can sometimes seem in hindsight, every company would be leading the charge. Instead, it takes hard work and strategic planning, and there are no guarantees. Indeed, as more companies try to stake out ground as sustainable firms, doing the right thing and making smart strategic moves that ultimately impact entire industries, it becomes harder to find the advantages that will truly last as meaningful wins. The landscape is constantly maturing and changing, the metrics are evolving, and the ingredients for success in this space can shift over time. There are ways organizations can approach these issues, and set themselves up to win, but before we explore what these efforts can involve for entire organizations, it's important to consider what they can sometimes mean for the individuals most affected.

THE PERSONAL CHALLENGE: A WASTE OF POTENTIAL

In December 2013, I visited Oslo, Norway, where I gave the keynote speech about the shift toward sustainable business practices and what it meant for people, for businesses, and for the planet. While there, I met Erik Osmundsen, the CEO of the largest waste management company in Norway. Erik was a year into his tenure as CEO of Norsk Gjenvinning, and he was excited about leading an organization that had the potential to make an enormous difference. Through recycling and other advances in the processing of materials, waste management companies can end up lowering carbon emissions and delivering huge environmental benefits. Erik was about to launch a massive effort to do this and was optimistic about the road ahead. However, the work did not unfold as Erik had initially hoped.

As Erik and I became friends, I witnessed his struggles moving an organization in the direction of sustainability and saw the challenges that face a leader who is genuinely concerned about business ethics, corruption, and the need to build a circular economy. Erik's tenure at NG began when the company's behavior—and, indeed, the whole industry's behavior—was not ideal from a social perspective. Soon after Erik started, he discovered instances of misconduct, ranging from some employees not recording small transactions at collection facilities and pocketing the cash to others mixing hazardous waste with nonhazardous waste and calling it all nonhazardous to minimize treatment costs. As he investigated further, he realized that these practices, which jeopardized human health and an open society, actually ran rampant throughout the industry.

Disappointed, and motivated to change things, Erik issued an ultimatum to his employees: act with the highest ethical standards, in accordance with the principles of sustainability, or leave the company. As it turned out, many employees were not on board, and they chose to leave (or were fired). Unfortunately, this did not solve the problem, at least not in a way that helped the business. Some departing employees took customers with them, tremendously harming the business. More than 60 percent of NG's line managers left within two years. Erik could not replace them quickly enough, and he hired people from outside the industry (not an easy sell) in order to find people who weren't inured to the poor industry practices and could bring a better perspective to the situation.

Erik finally decided that the best way to change things would be to go public and speak to the media. The effort backfired. The whole industry, including most of his competitors, denounced Erik's actions and isolated him. Given that his business goals threatened the power of organized crime (which had been paid by companies to take hazardous waste and illegally dump it in underdeveloped areas), Erik also got death threats. He was up at night obsessing about the safety of his wife and kids. "Should I be doing this?" he asked himself. "Am I the right person to take this on?"

It was not the corporate turnaround he envisioned. He told my Harvard Business School class in the spring of 2021 that it wasn't the life he expected. He needed a security detail to protect him, and his family was frightened by the threats he received. Erik kept telling himself that this was a moment in his life when he had to make sacrifices in order to potentially make a great impact on the world. He was fortunate to have a board of directors that was behind him, and to be living and working in a country with good police protection, transparency, and a legal framework that supported him. He convinced another company to come out in favor of reform, so that he was not fighting the battle alone. Nevertheless, it was very challenging, extremely difficult on a personal level, and emblematic of how putting these efforts into practice is not always simple, even when you believe the data and have every good intention.

Erik's story is an extreme example—not every leader gets death threats—but it illuminates the kinds of challenges many leaders have faced over the past decade when trying to implement change in industries or at companies that aren't quite ready for it. They have experienced extreme pushback, skepticism, isolation, and even attacks as they have worked to create change. Even though there is now profound evidence that over the long term integrating ESG issues into strategy can be a winning proposition, that isn't always enough. NG is on track to achieve record financial performance in 2021, but Erik understood when he started on this path that there were no guarantees. Individual leaders incur tremendous personal costs, and even when they succeed, they end up working far harder than they would have otherwise. There is no free lunch.

THE CORPORATE CHALLENGE: CRAWL BEFORE YOU RUN

We have absolutely progressed as a society over the past generation from companies doing almost nothing when it came to ESG efforts to something far more mature. However, getting there has been slow. When ESG data first started to percolate into the mainstream, it was used largely to judge a company's ability to avoid harm and its general willingness to do good. It was a signal to the market that a leader wanted to achieve positive outcomes for society and the environment, but there was little specificity, and no indication of how the efforts might fit into a strategic vision. ESG performance was about good intentions, but not really about the output. Advice for how a company could maximize the impact of sustainability efforts would have perhaps centered on website language and a well-crafted press release.

Now, it involves much more than that. More and more is being measured, and the only way to maintain an advantage and out-perform the competition is by achieving real results, making ESG issues core to a business, going above and beyond the competition, and measuring and communicating amazing results. All of these things are hard for almost any company to do well.

Nevertheless, my research and the research of my colleagues has found that effectively reaping rewards from sustainability in the current environment—doing good and simultaneously excel-ling in terms of financial results—isn't just guesswork. There is a defined path and a framework companies can turn to in order to guide decision-making.

HOW TO GET TO SUSTAINABLE INNOVATION

The path is intuitive, to some extent. You have to crawl before you can run. Companies go through three stages before achieving sustainable innovation (see figure 5.1). The first is about compliance. They think of ESG as a series of boxes they have to tick off to avoid a bad outcome. These include simple actions, simple disclosures, events, and marketing and publicity that borders on goodwashing. In the past, this was enough. Today, these are table stakes, required just to be in the game.

FIGURE 5.1

McDonald's, for example, announced not long ago that in response to public concern about the proliferation of plastic straws—one estimate found more than 500 million straws used each day in the United States alone, and perhaps as many as 8.3 billion straws washing up on beaches around the world—the company would ban straws in the United Kingdom and Ireland. At the same time, Starbucks announced its own global phaseout of plastic straws. These are fine moves, but they are reactive, and quite possibly were undertaken only because the cost of doing so was relatively minimal for these companies. They are not part of a broader strategy and are largely all about the headlines. This is the kind of activity typical of a company in the early stages of sustainable behavior. Efforts are scattershot, rarely driven by an overall strategic imperative, often employee-driven, voluntary, and in response to pressures from outside.

Next, companies move to the efficiency stage. There, they find the low-hanging fruit; for example, reducing carbon emissions or strengthening community relationships. They invest money and time, but it is simply a reallocation of existing resources, cherry-picking the kinds of efforts they want to pursue; any competitive advantage gained is short-lived. Efficiency activities are becoming common practice for companies at this stage, necessary for survival but not capable of differentiating one company from another. Twenty years ago, announcing a goal of carbon neutrality would have been revolutionary. Today, it is pretty standard. Here, actions are still at the periphery of what the core business is about, and might include such things as establishing a separate department around safety or the supply chain or creating stand-alone programs area by area. While it is absolutely good news that companies are undertaking these efforts, they are not at a point where they're able to get lasting advantages that don't get competed away.

The third stage is about innovation. Here is where companies become great. This stage is not just about changing bits of the company's behavior, such as improving the energy efficiency in the production of environmentally inferior legacy products like internal combustion engine vehicles; instead, it is about transforming the entire company, in this case perhaps developing new core capabilities to produce affordable and technically attractive electric vehicles.

THE DIFFERENTIATOR:
STEPS TOWARD MEANINGFUL INNOVATION

How do you get to that stage? How do you find sustainable innovations that are worth the hard work and investment? For this, my research identifies a five-action framework for management:

- Find and adopt the ESG practices that will be most strategic;
- Create smart ESG goals and accountability structures;

- Build a culture around corporate purpose;
- Make the right operational changes for ESG success; and
- Communicate effectively to investors and the world.

Figure 5.2 illustrates this five-step path. We will spend the rest of this chapter examining each of these steps.

View ESG as a Strategy → Build Accountability → Build a Culture around Corporate Purpose → Design the Organization for Trust → Credibly Communicate Outcomes

FIGURE 5.2

BE STRATEGIC: THE SURPRISING POWER OF VASELINE

You would think that there is very little possibility to innovate when your product is a jar of petroleum jelly that has been around for almost 150 years. Nevertheless, not long ago, leaders at Vaseline looked for ways to differentiate themselves, and realized when talking to medical professionals that the product was a vital part of emergency first-aid kits around the world. This was especially true in developing countries, where the product could actually be the difference between people being able to go to work or school instead of being stuck at home with burns or cracked hands from cooking on open stoves or using kerosene lamps. The company developed a distribution strategy to help heal the skin of millions of people living in crisis or conflict—a brand differentiator and a smart social impact strategy.

We have covered the issue of materiality and figuring out the measures that matter in different industries. Strategic thinking is about predicting what's next; that is, determining what isn't yet on the world's radar screen but has the potential to be there soon, and identifying important industry drivers before the competition (or the SASB) does. If you can identify and adopt strategic ESG practices and make them core parts of your business before there is any external pressure to do so, you can find breakthrough ESG success.

For instance, IKEA has moved past its traditional positioning as the maker of inexpensive furniture that's bound to wind up in the trash to focusing its product design on reusable, recyclable, and refurbishable goods. Before the world forces the company to consider how much waste it produces, it is getting ahead of the curve, making modular products that can be dismantled and easily turned back into raw materials. In addition, IKEA is entering new businesses like solar energy.

Nike used the desire to reduce waste to inform its efforts to create the Flyknit shoe, which uses a single strand of yarn to create the entire upper section of the product. The product produces zero waste, is less expensive to manufacture than traditional footwear, and is ultimately a better shoe. Nike markets its use of high-strength fibers to create a more lightweight, breathable, and supportive piece of footwear. The Flyknit is responsible for more than $1 billion in sales so far, an innovation driven by sustainability concerns.

The list goes on and on. Xylem is a US-based company that has created sensor-driven software to find leaks in water pipes, improving the efficiency of our water system while inventing a brand-new business. Maersk, a Danish shipping company, redesigned its ships to reduce fuel consumption. Medical manufacturer Becton, Dickinson and Company created a safer syringe to help prevent the spread of HIV. Electric utility CLP Group (originally China Light and Power) moved into the alternative energy space. CVS Health distinguished itself from competitors by no longer selling cigarettes, and moving into the health care space by opening up medical clinics.

Finding the strategic openings that can enable innovation and at the same time improve performance on sustainability metrics is critical for success, but it's only the first piece of the puzzle.

CREATE GOALS AND ACCOUNTABILITY
STRUCTURES: TOP-DOWN AND BOTTOM-UP

You might have all the good intentions and even the right strategy, but the truth is that most strategic development efforts fail to be implemented, and even the ones that do get off the ground are not always well executed and don't always succeed. In my research, I've found that you need pressure from both ends—top-down and bottom-up—two forces pushing on the organization to make things work and to make them stick.

By top-down, I am talking about real accountability at the highest levels of the organization. Commitment must start with the board of directors and be diffused throughout a company. In most companies, the board of directors is far removed from ESG efforts. This is a problem. One of the characteristics most strongly tied to high ESG performance is board involvement. The board of directors is the ultimate governance vehicle in most organizations; even the most senior management is held accountable. We have found that strong governance engaged in sustainability issues is critical to success. The French international banking group BNP Paribas, for example, has directors who are leaders in sustainable finance, which helps give credence to the company's sustainability efforts.

Our research shows that the leaders of sustainable companies are simply different from their peers, in a number of respects (see figure 5.3). There are clear differences between leaders at these companies, and it manifests in the risks they will take to pursue sustainability and the operations changes they are willing to implement.

Another idea that often seems impactful, and has been tried by a number of companies, is linking executive pay to sustainability outcomes. Microsoft is an example of a company that has tied executive pay to increased workplace diversity, with one-sixth of CEO Satya Nadella's bonus (which was $10.8 million in 2019) tied to diversity goals. With diversity a critical issue in the technology

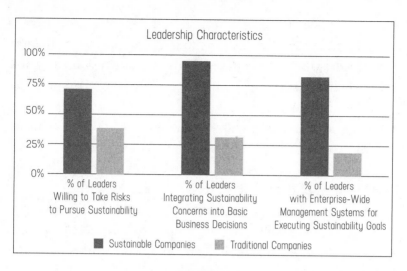

FIGURE 5.3

industry, to make sure products and services reflect the needs and interests of all populations, this decision shows real commitment by the Microsoft board. A number of large polluters in the energy space—BHP and Royal Dutch Shell, for example—have linked executive compensation to carbon emissions, with 20 to 25 percent of CEO bonuses tied to results.

It is interesting, and perhaps counterintuitive, that while monetary incentives can make a difference for relatively low-hanging fruit like the projects just mentioned, for more fundamental sustainability projects that require large investment or new operations structures, the motivations play out differently. To implement the kinds of innovative programs that ultimately make the biggest long-term difference, setting challenging targets, ambitious beyond cheap talk, can be the most powerful way to effectively galvanize energy throughout the organization.

In 2012, I wrote about Dow, the global advanced materials company. Dow had committed to a "Vision of Zero," setting a goal of not just reducing but eliminating accidents in their manufacturing plants. They had no idea how to achieve that, but imagined that the goal would mobilize the collective ingenuity of their engineers and other floor managers. Ultimately, they achieved the target, preventing an estimated thirteen thousand injuries over the course of a decade, and certainly improving workplace productivity and culture in the process.

After analyzing more than eight hundred corporate targets related to climate change with Jody Grewal from the University of Toronto and David Freiberg from the Impact-Weighted Accounts Initiative, the research revealed that audacious targets are far more likely to be met than modest ones.[1] Aiming high leads to more investment, more significant operating changes, more innovation, and more accountability. Setting tough goals makes them more likely to be reached than settling on more easily achievable aspirations. In these cases, monetary incentives have a negative effect, and reaching for the stars pays off.

The reason for this may have to do with culture, which is such a powerful force in business organizations. This is the kind of bottom-up thinking that has to go along with top-down dictates. Ambitious goals activate ambitious employees up and down the organization, and communicate that these outcomes matter. We now believe that when goals are hard to achieve, the stress imposed from tying achievement to compensation negates the positive effect. You need commitment at every level of an organization; you do not need fear. Motivation—namely, a positive willingness to innovate and change—is crucial, and it is the next piece of the puzzle.

CREATE A CULTURE AROUND
CORPORATE PURPOSE: SEEING THE LIGHT

Philips, which spun off its lighting division as a separate company, Signify, in 2018, has long been a leader in light bulbs. In recent years, however, it switched its focus from light bulbs with a limited life span to lighting as a sustainable service, with interactive LED lighting systems and sensor networks, and smart lighting for homes, offices, and even greenhouses. Now, 82.5 percent of the company's revenue comes from sustainable products, systems, and services, beating the goal Philips set to reach: 80 percent by 2020.

This change of purpose, going from providing a (wasteful) product to selling a (sustainable) service, can inspire employees (bottom-up thinking!) and create a corporate culture ready to rally around sustainability. Strategic efforts fail when people below the top of an organizational hierarchy don't sense true commitment or lack the direction they need to fulfill the aspiration.

I am reminded of the time a global clothing company invited me to its headquarters to better understand their sustainability strategy. I was fascinated by the commitment and emotional investment I sensed when I talked to the top executives at the firm. The next day, I visited middle managers in charge of procurement and workers on the front lines in the company's stores. With them, it was a very different story. As one employee told me: "The talk is all up there. Down here, there is only one purpose: sell to the customer what we have in inventory and what we can source at the lowest cost—not necessarily what the customer needs."

It's a stark example, but it helps illustrate the point. Purpose is critical—up and down an organization—and finding the right purpose, aligned with the ESG issues that have been identified as strategic and achievable, can be a huge part of the recipe for impact. Health care company Novo Nordisk builds a values framework into everything it does, balancing financial, social, and economic considerations. Brewing company Anheuser-Busch InBev infuses employee goals from top to bottom with sustainability considerations. They hope that investing employees in the company's goals makes them more likely to be achieved. The CEO of insurance company Aetna introduced employee wellness programs as an effort to focus the company's purpose around health and not just profit. And we have already discussed the transformation of Microsoft around purpose.

MAKE ESSENTIAL OPERATIONAL
CHANGES: DESIGN FOR TRUST

A strategic goal, accountability from the top down, and a top-to-bottom culture built around purpose are not always enough to actually get things done. The fourth piece of the puzzle is operational. The structure of a sustainable company needs to have sustainability infused into everything it does.

One type of thinking that I have seen drive this quality in several organizations is something the founders of Airbnb have called Designing for Trust. This mission enabled the company to go public in 2020 with a market capitalization exceeding $100 billion. What makes Airbnb possible, according to cofounder Joe Gebbia, isn't only the accommodations themselves; it is the culture of trust, which has to permeate every aspect of the company's operations. Guests need to trust hosts in order to want to stay in their homes. Hosts need to trust guests in order to allow them to stay there. Both sides need to trust that the company is a backstop of safety, and that it will be there to mediate disputes and handle any problems that arise. Without fully embedding that principle into the organization, announcing your amazing business model where people will bring strangers into their homes and pay you a fee for the privilege of doing so sounds almost absurd.

Uber's model draws on many of the same ideas. Getting into a car with a stranger late at night . . . that idea doesn't work without very deliberate choices made to foster trust. These companies don't just talk about safety on the periphery of their business; they make very clear decisions at every stage of the product, and at every level of the company, from the CEO on down. It is embedded into the DNA.

While neither Airbnb nor Uber are necessarily thought of as sustainability leaders, their emphasis on trust has allowed them to create entirely new ways for us to operate our houses and our cars. Trust is at the core of sustainability. Trust allows companies to implement new strategies, and also becomes the outcome of successful implementation. Trust leads to the ability to become more sustainable, and becoming more sustainable inevitably leads to greater trust.

What's interesting to note is that Airbnb and Uber weren't reinventing old ways of doing business at their organizations. They were starting from scratch, making it much easier to infuse customer satisfaction and value into every piece of what they do. Engineering operational change for a legacy company, with systems already in place and a business model that already works, is a different kind of process. What my research shows is that just as a company needs to crawl before it can run, moving to an actual operational structure that focuses on positive impact can look less like a sudden all-in change and more like an evolution (figure 5.4 illustrates this point).

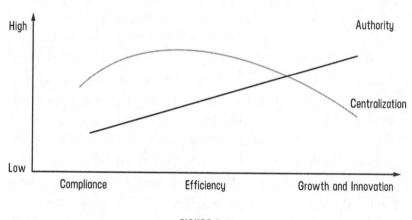

FIGURE 5.4

As you can see, the path starts with the establishment and growth of an authority for sustainability. Typically someone is designated to be in charge of ESG efforts—sometimes a CSO (chief sustainability officer), though often it is a lower-level officer at first, perhaps a sustainability manager. These people begin to coordinate sustainability efforts, which can start from a very immature and decentralized position, scattershot throughout the company, driven by individual employees who happen to have an interest or motivation to pursue particular goals, and without much CEO involvement. The employees initially put in charge of sustainability often do not have much authority, and come from a range of backgrounds. Often they have already engaged in some ESG work, perhaps as part of their previous role. They become the advocates that move the organization to the next stage and beyond.

Once sustainability is established as a goal, these officers can start to consolidate power and coordinate the company's efforts. They usually begin by reducing waste and increasing resource efficiency, and engage more and more internal stakeholders in the mission, marshaling support that will be useful as the efforts grow. Hans Wegner, the CSO of National Geographic, one of the largest educational and scientific nonprofits in the world, described (in the research my colleagues and I performed) how, while National Geographic was reporting on climate and other social issues, as an organization it wasn't playing its part to help the planet. Wegner got sign-off from the CEO of the company for a new, sustainable vision, set targets for zero waste, carbon neutrality, and improved employee health. He built the business case for these initiatives, and helped shepherd the organization into the next phase of sustainability.

I teach my classes about JetBlue, the airline founded in 1998 with a mission to "bring humanity back to air travel." In 2011, the company realized it could be doing more on the sustainability front and saw itself falling behind on issues like recycling. They were throwing away one hundred million cans a year and had no onboard recycling program in place. A head of sustainability, Sophia Mendelsohn, was hired to lead the company's efforts. She tried to engage with managers in every department, as well as with the investor relations group, in order to understand the landscape in which she would be working. She launched small projects at first—decreasing water use during engine washings and moving to paperless cabins, for example—to earn some quick wins and get more visibility and buy-in across the company.

Next, she went big. She tied the company's core business to sustainability goals and signed the biggest deal in history for the procurement of renewable jet fuel through a long-term agreement (at a cost competitive with traditional jet fuel). This decreased both carbon emissions and the volatility of the airline's largest-cost item.

Tying sustainability issues to the bigger picture, as Mendelsohn did, is how companies move to the last stage, where after spending some time centralizing power in a senior-level CSO, they now have to decentralize their efforts and move them back into the entire organization. It is perhaps counterintuitive that a company must first put energy into establishing a department dedicated to sustainability and coordinating efforts around a single leader, giving him or her the authority to get things done, to only then turn around and dismantle that structure, and give responsibility back to the individual business functions, and cede centralized decision-making. But it makes sense if you think about it. If you want to develop a greener product, you need the product developers to be executing that vision, not a separate sustainability department. If you want to improve conditions across your supply chain, you need everyone working within that chain to be paying attention, not just one outside division that isn't there in the trenches.

This is something many companies struggle with, and it's why meaningful innovation is hard. Decentralization is one of the trickiest challenges for a company, because the head of finance, for instance, isn't necessarily used to thinking about ESG issues. The head of research and development isn't used to prioritizing the needs of the planet. The heads of every department have their own agenda, their own expertise, and their own to-do lists. Keeping ESG concerns at the top of that list—not just for one person charged with thinking about those issues, but for everyone charged with thinking about everything within the company—is a huge endeavor and ties back to the idea of culture and trust. Delegation of important decisions cannot happen in a low-trust environment. It cannot happen in a culture where there is backstabbing and dishonesty. It's a by-product of meaningful, corporate purpose diffused throughout the organization. It is exactly the kind of progress that leads to true competitive advantage, and it can only emerge when there is a barrier to imitation. It can only emerge when something is difficult to copy. Doing this well is what makes companies great.

COMMUNICATE TO INVESTORS
AND THE WORLD: VITAL INFORMATION

The final link in the chain is about communication. The reality is that some of these sustainability benefits take a long time to accrue. Transformational change can take years or even decades to show results, and that is a challenge, especially in an environment that favors short-term reporting and quarterly earnings declarations. CEOs committed to growing sustainable organizations that can thrive over time need to resist short-termism. The easiest way to do that is the most straightforward: they need to talk about long-term goals. My research indicates that few companies do this, despite expressing concerns about "quarterly capitalism." They need to actually provide insight to investors about their long-term thinking and the reasons they chose to invest in sustainability.

Companies can influence who invests and what investors want. They can shape the discussion and encourage long-term-oriented investors to come their way. The UK-based biotechnology company Shire did just this leading up to its acquisition by Takeda Pharmaceutical Company in 2019. The company integrated ESG issues into its strategy and its reporting, and found that institutional investors known to be dedicated to long-term holdings increased their holdings—until they in fact held more shares than transient investors who would be more resistant to long-term thinking.

Companies need to build relationships and trust with investors, and this is where so many organizations fail massively. They disclose a few general ideas and think that's enough, but that doesn't work. It's not about intermittent, piecemeal disclosure, but about an ongoing conversation, an evolving set of ideas, and a complete and transparent set of reports. If you are disrupting an existing market—like Tesla with electric cars or Oatly in the alternative milk space—there will be vicissitudes, and things that don't work or take more time than expected. Explaining why you are doing things differently and why you think competitive advantage will result in the end is critical for keeping investors (and the media, and customers, and employees) on board and supportive.

We have covered the range of communication tools out there, from adopting standards like those from SASB, to communicating material issues, to moving to integrated reporting and impact-weighted accounting, and the kinds of signaling that companies can do to show that they are committed to these issues. Of course, disclosure has to be consistent and complete. It cannot be selective, highlighting only the positives while obscuring the negatives, and it cannot be done in a way that makes it impossible to judge differences across firms. The point of disclosure is to show progress, and also to make effective comparisons.

Sophia Mendelsohn at JetBlue, once confident in her efforts across the company, acted to increase sustainability reporting, making the voluntary move to follow SASB guidelines, and using its set of industry-specific issues material to the airline industry to drive further change. The company was the first airline to install sharklets (curved extensions at wing tips, also known as winglets) on its planes to improve fuel efficiency and lower their environmental footprint. She also worked to begin the transition to renewable jet fuel, and improve employee training and recognition. JetBlue also became the first airline to commit to making climate-related financial disclosures. Within just a few years, the company engineered a complete shift in both its efforts and its communication about those efforts.

Chief Executives for Corporate Purpose is an organization I have worked with to help CEOs develop strategies to communicate long-term plans and demonstrate how they have integrated ESG issues into their companies. In just two years, more than forty leaders of large corporations—ranging from UPS to IBM to Aetna—have used the framework to communicate to investors with more than $25 trillion in assets under management how their strategies are competitive in the long term and create tremendous value for society. In the end, it is not just about releasing data, it is about actively spreading the message, through every possible outlet. The measurement and reporting tools that CECP provides can be a start, but the messaging has to infuse everything a company does.

In the best cases, companies can move to change corporate status. Becoming a B Corp or a benefit corporation can do a tremendous amount to signal to investors, customers, employees, and any other stakeholders that these issues matter and are driving the business decisions being made behind the scenes. Vital Farms, an ethical producer of eggs and butter, is one example of a company that has put all of the pieces together. Its purpose is clear in everything it does—with "We're on a mission to bring ethically produced food to the table" splashed prominently across its website, along with messaging about commitment to animal welfare, employees, customers, climate change, and the world. The company, which works with two hundred family farms around the country, originally incorporated in Texas in 2009 and became a public benefit corporation in 2017. "Every hen is humanely treated," it shares on its website. "Every egg is pasture-raised and we continue to elevate our (and the industry's) standards, continuing [founder] Matt [O'Hayer]'s commitment to ethics over profits."[2] Matt O'Hayer and I spoke at the same event in 2020. He told me: "Our products are not only better for society but they also taste better. People love them." That combination has been the formula for success. In just a few years, Vital Farms has gone from a small farm business to a company with a market value exceeding $1 billion.

Even the smallest companies can make these issues a priority, and make communication an element of their strategy in multiple directions. Burlap & Barrel is a Public Benefit Corporation with just three full-time employees on a mission to deliver single-origin culinary spices, like cinnamon, nutmeg, chili peppers, and others, to the world. The supply chain for most spices is long and complicated, with spices from many farmers in many countries ending up mixed together, top-quality product mixed with subpar filler, and the spices getting older and older as they travel from warehouse to warehouse and finally to the grocery store, sometimes with as many as twenty stops along the way. Burlap & Barrel shortens the chain dramatically, working directly with its partner farmers to bring recently harvested spices directly to its customers. By cutting out the middlemen, the company can pay its partner farmers two to ten times the typical commodity prices, while customers get a higher quality, unadulterated product and still pay prices similar to what they might pay in the grocery store.

Each year, the company issues a social impact report, outlining how it is helping its partner farmers around the world. By providing farmers with more income for their spices than they can get on the commodity market, and working with them to take on more pieces of the supply chain (for example, doing their own cleaning, sorting, and drying of the spices and preparing them for export), Burlap & Barrel allows the farmers to have far more agency to decide what to grow and how to grow it. The company shares the story of one farmer, Don Amilcar Pereira, whose life has been a journey from picking cardamom to owning the only vertically integrated cardamom farm in Guatemala, growing and drying his own spices, transporting and packing them, and becoming both a farmer and a full-fledged entrepreneur supporting his local community.

Moreover, it's not only about the social impact. "The social impact story is the bonus, but the more important piece is connecting that impact to how it enables customers to have access to far more flavorful ingredients," explains Burlap & Barrel cofounder Ori Zohar.[3] What is particularly interesting about the company's story is how the social mission changes the way it communicates not just with its customers, but with its farmers, and how this in turn improves the product.

"Farmers typically have no visibility into who is consuming their spices, and how they're consuming them," says Zohar, "and this can have a massive impact on what they're growing. We give them information they need to make a more delicious product."[4] On the commodity market, he explains, spices are often graded by color and size, which might have very little relationship to flavor. Don Amilcar Perreira had been selling big, green cardamom pods—the only kind the market was demanding. The direct relationship he formed with Burlap & Barrel led them to a riper version of cardamom, yellow in color, with a fruity and floral aroma and a sweeter flavor—a more interesting spice for customers even if most commercial buyers weren't interested.

Perreira also enticed the company to buy another crop, sun-dried black limes, popular in the Middle East but unusual in the United States. Building on the public's increasing interest in Mediterranean and Middle Eastern cooking, the product became a hit with home cooks, making it among the top five most popular spices the company sells. If not for the direct relationship the company had built with its partner farmers, Burlap & Barrel would not have known its partner was growing the spice, customers would have missed out, and Perreira would have lost out on a significant source of income. Communication, resulting from the social mission, ends up driving the business in multiple ways.

WORK WELL DONE: THE REWARD

Putting everything together gets us back to the numbers: a premium of greater than 3 percent in the financial markets for companies that find a way to lead with sustainability. It is not easy, but with a concerted effort, putting together strategy, accountability, culture, operational focus, and effective communication, companies big and small can reap the benefits of alignment and serve the world while they also become leaders in their industries.

In the next chapter, we will examine how companies can think about these efforts in terms of the larger picture. Where does this 3 percent emerge from, and how are companies reaping that gain? In other words, why are successful sustainability outcomes successful? I have identified six archetypes of opportunity that successful companies take advantage of, and that is where we turn next.

Chapter Six

THE ARCHETYPES OF OPPORTUNITY: HOW COMPANIES CAPTURE VALUE

As I have shared the stories of different companies throughout this book, you may be noticing some common themes: companies shifting their current business models; companies launching brand-new businesses; companies changing their internal processes to coincide with evolving societal expectations and norms; and so on. These are not scattershot efforts—there are ways to organize them so as to present a map to business leaders and investors demonstrating the various ways companies find opportunities to win through alignment.

In this chapter, I cover how I think of these efforts, and explain the six archetypes that I have codified. Together, they represent the vast majority, if not the totality, of the ways companies are capturing value by doing good. As I see it, successful companies find success by pursuing six categories of opportunity:

1. *New Model and/or Market:* Growing revenue through new environmental or socially minded products and initiatives, often aimed at new markets, where these new endeavors can end up driving what the business stands for in the marketplace.
2. *Business Transformation:* Shifting an existing misaligned business into a different type of product or service, with far greater alignment.

3. *Pure Play Aligned:* Launching a brand-new business built on a model that emerges directly from new environmental or social considerations.

4. *Substitute Product:* Existing products becoming superior to their competitors because of characteristics that gain prominence, in light of broader environmental or social issues in the world.

5. *Operational Efficiencies:* Improving return on capital through ESG-focused initiatives that save money by decreasing a company's environmental footprint, increasing worker productivity, or other similar outcomes.

6. *Recognizing Value:* Moving in the shadow of ESG leaders in the industry, using the recognition the leaders are getting to drive an increase in market valuation multiple.

These categories do not all share the same risk of failure or potential degree of disruption to the status quo. The first three offer particularly high upside potential, but also come with significant risks. The second three offer lower potential for breakthrough outcomes, but also serve as lower-risk ways to meaningfully increase value. Figure 6.1, where the y-axis represents the potential value creation and the x-axis represents implementation risk, illustrates this.

On the graph, you can see the six archetypes. The shaded boxes show the archetypes that relate principally to new entrants and entrepreneurial efforts (although in some cases we also see legacy companies creating new markets or developing/acquiring pure plays). The dotted lines represent opportunities for established and legacy businesses. The remaining two represent archetypes for both established and new businesses.

Needless to say, there are differences within each of the archetypes in terms of both potential value creation and implementation risk. For example, one pure play aligned effort could easily be higher in terms of both value creation and risk than another in a way that makes the potential value creation exceed what is happening in a business transformation. In other words, those archetypes can blend into one another in terms of both value creation and implementation risk.

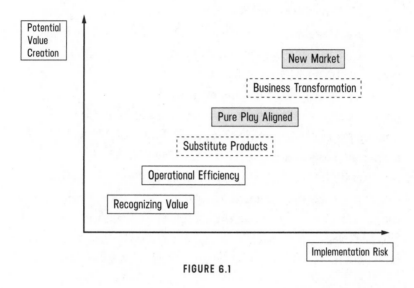

FIGURE 6.1

What follows is a case study from each of these categories to illustrate how these archetypes actually play out in the real world, and what you can do to pursue each of them.

NEW MODEL AND/OR MARKET: SEEING THE FUTURE

Value doesn't have to emerge from every element of the business if the mission can align with social trends and bring new customer markets along. This archetype relates to companies that make their environmental and social impact so prominent that it becomes synonymous with the very product or service they offer, and drives their growth.

The apparel business does not necessarily have to align with social goals, but the outdoor clothing brand Patagonia made it so, with its commitment to environmental protection. The automobile business suffers from its association with pollution and negative environmental impacts, but car manufacturer Tesla reached out to new audiences with its zero-emission vehicles. The eyeglass retailer Warby Parker emphasizes the social good of glasses, in a space that was devoid of innovation for generations, by providing eyewear to underserved populations and making this effort a key part of its business.

In Warby Parker's case, the eyeglass business itself has no special characteristics that make sustainability an imperative (though helping people see better is obviously a huge social good), but the company has chosen to let social mission drive profits. This decision made the business appealing to a new group of customers motivated by those issues. In the process, it has uncovered a new market that can help spread the company's name and brand globally. For every pair of glasses sold, Warby Parker distributes a pair of glasses to a person in need. In the company's view, it is decidedly not charity. "We view our investment in our social mission as having an incredibly high ROI over a long timeframe," cofounder and co-CEO Dave Gilboa told *Forbes* magazine.[1]

For Warby Parker, it's not merely a donation; the effort must include deeper involvement. The program drives the business in many ways. For example, it sends many employees on trips to work with their nonprofit partners to distribute the glasses, so these employees can see firsthand the effect that the company is having on local communities in the developing world. Gilboa firmly believes that the social mission of the company is a competitive differentiator, making Warby Parker resonate with employees and customers—just like the trend toward aligning corporate purpose with consumer and employee desires that we explored in chapter two. As societal attitudes have evolved, these initiatives are how companies like Warby Parker develop consumer loyalty, and grow fans over time.

Earlier, I wrote about Unilever and its commitment to healthier brands and products. It is another example in this category; one element of the business drives alignment, and the company uses it to stand out and become a market leader.

BUSINESS TRANSFORMATION: PUTTING ENERGY INTO SUSTAINABLE CHANGE

In the face of emerging environmental or social issues, many companies feel forced to try to entirely transform their businesses. Unfortunately, as my Harvard Business School colleague Professor Rebecca Henderson has extensively written, such corporate transformations are rarely successful. Think about the failure of Kodak to adapt from analog to digital photography, or Nokia's move from mobile phones to smartphones. More recently, we have seen many legacy automobile manufacturers struggle to adapt from internal combustion engine vehicles to electric models, and from selling cars to selling transportation as a service.

There are many obstacles in the way when companies try to enact a wholesale transformation, whether it is new infrastructure requirements, the difficulties of retraining employees, cultural issues, organizational inertia, or the loss of whatever nontransferable competitive advantages were making the initial business a success. However, for the few that succeed, the benefits can be overwhelming.

If you only watch the beautiful videos of lush, clean landscapes and seascapes produced by the Finnish company Neste, with windmills spinning in the bright blue sky, you would never know that, until recently, it was a company built around oil refining and marketing. If you were in northeast Germany in 2008, as the Danish firm DONG Energy fought to develop a massive coal-fired power plant, you wouldn't believe that a little more than a decade later, that same company would become the global leader in offshore wind power, with a new name (Ørsted) and a completely new business.

Both Neste and Ørsted have embraced the idea that the future of energy has to be clean. Neste has become the world's largest producer of renewable diesel and jet fuel and is committed to carbon neutrality by 2035, focused on what it calls innovative, circular solutions to reuse carbon again and again. The company was ranked fourth on the Corporate Knights 2021 Global 100 Most Sustainable Companies list, its fourth consecutive year in the top four.[2]

Two spots above it on the 2021 list—and coming off a number one ranking in 2020—is Ørsted in nearby Denmark. In 2009, as DONG Energy, 85 percent of the company's heat and power came from coal. That year, it set a goal of reversing the split by 2040—85 percent from renewable sources. It beat its target by an astonishing twenty-one years, declaring in 2019 that 86 percent of its energy was generated by renewables, and that it was now the world's largest offshore wind power provider.

For Ørsted, it all started when opposition to a proposed new coal plant in Germany caused the project to fail. "This was the first clear sign telling us the world was beginning to move in a different direction," Martin Neubert, the CEO of Ørsted's offshore-wind business, told McKinsey in 2020.[3]

"We discussed what our future growth areas should be," Neubert explains, "areas where we had critical mass, where we had the right competences, and where we could differentiate ourselves. It became clear that one was wind power, which three of the six companies that merged to become DONG Energy in 2006 had already pursued."[4]

They pivoted the business in that direction, with a team of more than fifty people working on renewable energy projects, and made a real effort to overcome the internal pressure to keep the business the way it had always been. Neubert describes how the employees felt that they were the world's best at coal—and didn't want to switch. Then gas prices dropped in the United States, changing the financials, and suddenly the shift to wind became easier to accept.

Ørsted has now divested itself from the oil and gas business, and will exit coal by 2023. It plans to be carbon-neutral by 2025, and is on the lookout for more ways to embrace sustainability. "Scanning new horizons and spotting new business areas are essential to Ørsted's strategy," Neubert declares.[5]

In the meantime, Ørsted's investors have been paid handsomely for the firm's transformation. In the five years leading up to March 2021, the company's stock was up more than 300 percent in a period when most energy stocks experienced negative returns. Neste's stock price rose by almost 400 percent. These are huge victories.

Many emerging opportunities fall into this category: incumbents that form a new strategic vision and combine it with true capability to pivot their products and services to new growth areas aligned with emerging environment and social issues. This archetype may offer the highest risk, but it also provides the greatest opportunities for massive success.

PURE PLAY ALIGNED: CONQUERING NEW LANDS

You may not have an existing business to transition into a new space; instead, alignment may lead to an entirely new business, operating under a model that would never before have made sense. Cultivo is a Mexican company that developed sophisticated artificial intelligence technology to analyze satellite imaging and find distressed farmland.

Founded by Manuel Piñuela, who holds a doctorate in electrical engineering, the company pinpoints areas that could be far more productive with better farming practices; for example, soil regeneration. This regenerated soil improves carbon absorption, creating carbon offsets that Cultivo sells to companies looking to manage their carbon footprint. Much of the cash from these transactions goes back into the pockets of the small farmers, who thereby gain from Cultivo's investment in making their land more productive, and they generate this brand-new, carbon-offset income stream. A win-win-win for farmers, Cultivo, and the planet.

Manuel told me that over the next five years, Cultivo's goal is to deploy $1 billion and restore at least 3.5 million hectares of land by financing a diverse range of projects, including projects involving forests, grasslands, wetlands, and regenerative agriculture. This is an ambitious goal, but there is also a large opportunity space. Out of the close to seven hundred million people across the globe living in extreme poverty, a large number of them are small farmers. Creating a new income stream for this population can provide an incredible mechanism for alleviating poverty and improving the lives of millions of families.

In addition, to avoid the most catastrophic consequences from climate change, as a planet we need to reach net-zero emissions by the middle of this century. Doing so will require negative-emissions solutions, meaning the absorption of more carbon from the air than we produce. We can do this with technological methods, such as carbon capture and storage, or through nature-based solutions, such as preserving forests and restoring the absorbing capacity of soil. Many companies have tried to innovate on the technology side. Cultivo is using technology to help innovate on the side of nature. Manuel believes that nature-based solutions have the potential to help achieve at least 30 percent of the carbon-emission-reduction goals by 2030, yet they currently receive only around 3 percent of the funding allocated to carbon capture. Cultivo's mission is to bridge this funding gap and unlock investment into opportunities that restore nature, protect livelihoods, and deliver healthy financial returns to investors, as Cultivo did in northern Mexico, where it sold carbon offsets from a grassland project to Aeroméxico, giving investors a significant return.

Another example in a similar space is AppHarvest, a public benefit corporation linking farmers and futurists, as the company likes to say. AppHarvest's technology allows indoor farms to produce more with less—using 90 percent less water and no chemical pesticides, with yields as much as thirty times greater than traditional farming, in a year-round crop cycle that creates twelve months of income. The company went public in 2021 and was valued at more than $1 billion, although it is still in its early stages.

Creating and sustaining these kinds of companies requires persistence, and sometimes even sacrificing some economic profit in the spirit of remaining true to their origins and mission. Not keeping the mission in mind would destroy the core competitive advantage of these firms, and the authentic connection between brand and product. At the same time, the "pure play" structure allows them to be laser-focused without having to worry about the liabilities of legacy misaligned businesses.

SUBSTITUTE PRODUCT: IT CAN BE DONE

Sometimes, you don't even need to change your product or your business, as shifting environmental and social concerns make some product attributes more and less appealing. This does not mean that nothing needs to be done. When an opportunity appears, the need to keep innovating in concert with the emerging environmental or social trend is extremely important. Ball Corporation, founded in 1880, began its history as a glass manufacturing company. It has diversified over the years and is now primarily one of the largest makers of recyclable aluminum beverage cans in the world. (The brand is still most familiar to consumers because of its home-canning products, most notably its glass canning jars—but Ball actually sold that part of the business in 1993 and licenses its trademark to the new owners.) Aluminum beverage cans have been around since the 1960s, but their popularity has waxed and waned. In the 1990s, demand slowed as more and more soft drinks moved to plastic bottles and the rise of craft breweries expanded the use of glass.[6] As society has recognized the problem of plastic pollution, there has been a resurgence in the use of aluminum.

Disposable plastic can take up to four hundred years to break down, with eight million tons of plastic waste dumped into the planet's oceans every year (the equivalent of five trash bags of plastic per foot of global coastline).[7] Fish, seabirds, and other animals are being strangled by plastic, or ingesting it to the detriment of their health. Once loose in the water, the plastic breaks down into tiny microplastics, which are impossible to retrieve. With this information becoming known, there has been a recent push away from plastic and back to aluminum cans, which are infinitely recyclable at a relatively low cost. (Although the bauxite mining required to produce aluminum is a very carbon-intensive process, if a company can create a circular model where the aluminum is recycled, then the overall environmental profile turns out to be quite friendly.)

This shift gave companies like Ball resurgent life in a previously fading industry. Seventy percent of new beverage launches are now in aluminum cans—most notably the growing market for seltzer and hard seltzer products—up from 30 percent just a few years ago. Ball is suddenly being seen as an ESG leader even though its core product has not changed from what it had been before.

All of that said, it is not enough to simply allow good fortune to transform your business into something that is now seen as socially responsible. As recently as 2011, the "Toxic 100" list from the Political Economy Research Institute at the University of Massachusetts Amherst[8] listed Ball as one of the top one hundred corporate air polluters in the United States. Since then, the company has committed to sustainability in a way it never had before. Ball has become the first can manufacturer to set science-based emissions targets, promising a 55 percent reduction in carbon emissions by the year 2030.[9] It anticipates a move to 100 percent renewable energy by 2022, and *Forbes* ranked it number one on its list of America's top companies for diversity. As one portfolio manager told me in 2020, the company is now a "must own" for any sustainability fund.

Of course, Ball did not passively ride this shift away from plastic. The company invested in real innovation to make the cans lighter, more recyclable, and resealable in a way that made them far more consumer-friendly. As a result, in the five years leading up to March 2021, Ball's stock was up more than 140 percent (as compared to the S&P 500's 88 percent rise over the same time frame).

If you can find a way to highlight the sustainable features of your product, and move your company in a direction that embraces them, the story of Ball shows that you can truly transform yourself into an ESG leader. A whole set of companies fall into this category, with their products providing a substitute to others that cause emerging environmental and social concerns. They can strategically exploit that shift in order to grow revenue and expand operations.

OPERATIONAL EFFICIENCY: DRIVING VALUE

This archetype is perhaps less exciting than the others, but it also offers the most broadly applicable solutions for most businesses. It is not always necessary to fundamentally change what you do, if you are able to find ways to run your business more efficiently, especially when those new efficiencies coincide with the environmental and social shifts going on in society. Thousands of companies have now learned what one of the largest advanced materials companies in the world learned two decades ago: environmental and social efforts can save money and make an organization more efficient and productive.

Earlier I wrote about the chemicals giant Dow. What impresses me about the company is its ability to drive toward highly significant and meaningful environmental, safety, and health goals while at the same time delivering massive efficiency gains—even in what was known to be a "difficult" industry with a history of pollution and accidents.[10]

Achieving their goals required the investment of $1 billion between 1996 and 2005—but that investment generated an overall value more than five times higher. Not only did their ambitious targets lead to 13,000 injuries avoided, but there were also 10,500 fewer leaks, breaks, and spills from its processes than would have otherwise occurred. The amount of solid waste produced by the company was reduced by 1.6 billion pounds (equivalent to a pile of waste one meter tall across approximately 415 football fields); water use dropped by 183 billion pounds (equivalent to the annual water usage of 170,000 US households); and energy use fell by 900 trillion BTUs (equivalent to the annual usage of 8 million US households).

Those efficiency gains continue to the present day. Dow's new set of goals, launched for the period between 2015 and 2025, has achieved $500 million in avoided costs as of 2020. As just one example, in Brazil, the company's excavation to install new brine wells resulted in unstable and unsafe embankments. Instead of a complete re-excavation, or a traditional "hard armor approach" using steel and concrete, Dow stabilized the embankments with local, readily available stone and reinforced vegetation. By creating this "living wall," Dow saved money compared to the alternative options, while also shrinking carbon emissions by 90 percent as well as reducing the impact to the local forest.

It is not so much that Dow had to change its business in a fundamental way, but rather that the company was able to shift its mission, set goals, and then find improvement upon improvement to make related efficiency gains that added up to billions of dollars over time.

RECOGNIZING VALUE: AHEAD OF THE MARKET

This last archetype concerns companies that have created value through their social and environmental alignment, but have not yet found this value reflected in their market capitalization. The hidden value here is especially relevant for investors. By identifying these companies before others see them, you put yourself in a position to achieve huge gains once the value is recognized more broadly and there is an expansion of valuation multiples.

We'll go much deeper in the next chapter on the importance of thinking about value for money from an investment perspective, but increasing the valuation of a company has other important effects in addition to making investors (and note that we are all investors through our pension money) more wealthy. To the extent that companies provide broad-based stock incentive plans or stock ownership plans, increasing the value of a company creates wealth for a large number of employees. It also allows aligned companies to use their shares as a currency to expand and do even more good for the world, either through better financing terms or by using their higher-valued shares as a currency to acquire companies.

The stories of NextEra Energy and AES, two electric utilities, are illustrative here. Both companies have made significant progress over time in developing a portfolio of renewable energy generation projects. This has allowed the companies to protect themselves against regulatory risk from the increased price of carbon emissions; it has also helped them foster new, more sustainable products and services to customers.

In moving their business in a more sustainable direction, NextEra attracted significant attention and became an investor favorite. The *Financial Times* described NextEra as the world's largest clean energy group, and the media gave them plenty of press as they passed oil and gas giant ExxonMobil in market capitalization.[11] In contrast, for a long time there was very little written about the efforts of AES, perhaps because of its smaller size. However, AES was a world leader in battery-based energy storage and in recent years became the fifth-largest solar developer in the world.[12]

Between 2016 and early 2020, the two companies had very similar stock price performance—but by mid-2020, AES had a market capitalization of four times its operating income while NextEra had a market capitalization of thirty times operating income. This was a huge difference for companies in very similar spaces. As the market finally realized the value of AES's efforts, between mid-2020 and the end of the year, AES's stock price increased by more than 100 percent while in comparison NextEra's increased by just 30 percent.

This expansion in the market valuation and the multiples that a company is trading at is our last archetype in terms of how I see companies create value. Of course, for this to happen, the alignment needs to be real and signal either reduced risk for the company going forward or higher-than-expected growth. It is not so much that a company is changing in these cases, but that the market is finally discovering it.

THE ROLE OF INVESTORS: MORE THAN PROFIT ALONE

These six archetypes demonstrate how companies can find tremendous value in this new landscape where doing good can be a huge driver of success. As these archetypes have emerged, and the potential value creation has become clear, investors have become increasingly interested in understanding how they can leverage ESG data to make better decisions. In 2018, Amir Amel-Zadeh of Oxford University and I documented this increase in investor interest, showing that investors with approximately $31 trillion in assets under management were looking at ESG issues through this critical lens of risk and value creation.

However, as I will argue next, it is not just about investors watching from the sidelines seeking to benefit. The investment community is a critical player in keeping the alignment strong, and making sure these trends last. They have been the audience for so many of the metrics developed over the past decade, and they are the people whose understanding of this issue is so important. Investors play key roles in incentivizing companies to continue on the path of looking for sustainable improvements, and in holding them accountable when those efforts fail. They have a tremendous amount of power in ensuring there is more and more reason for companies to keep trying to do better.

Chapter Seven

INVESTORS DRIVING CHANGE: MORE THAN NEGATIVE SCREENING

In 2017, a shareholder resolution forced the energy giant Exxon-Mobil (against the recommendation of the company's board) to disclose the impact that increasing efforts to reduce climate change would have on its business. Passing with 62.2 percent of the votes, the resolution was a tremendous signal that shareholders care about environmental issues and aren't afraid to push companies in the direction of taking action on behalf of the planet.

It's interesting that only a year earlier, a similar resolution failed, garnering just 38 percent support. At the time, I wrote a short article about the significance of that vote, and predicted that Exxon-Mobil would likely see an increase in shareholder activism in the future. I did not realize then that the resolution would pass just a year later. Now, as I write this, shareholder activism at ExxonMobil has gone even further.

Engine No. 1 is an organization founded by Chris James, a successful tech investor, that is leading the charge for a shareholder campaign to overhaul ExxonMobil. Their website, Reenergize XOM (the ticker symbol for ExxonMobil), urges shareholders to push the company toward "growth areas including more significant investment in clean energy . . . [and a commitment] to emission reduction targets."[1] As Chris told me, the company is a great example where change could benefit both shareholders and stakeholders because historically both had suffered: the company has experienced large negative stock returns over the past few years, as it has released an enormous quantity of carbon emissions. Changing that—moving to clean energy—would benefit the company, shareholders, and the environment. In a stunning result, Engine No. 1 board director nominees gained three board seats at Exxon-Mobil's 2021 annual general meeting, with shareholders voting against the recommendations of corporate management.

The events unfolding at ExxonMobil aren't outliers. In October 2020, 67 percent of the shareholders of multinational consumer goods company Procter & Gamble (one of the fifty largest companies in the world) voted in favor of a proposal to limit deforestation in its supply chain, going against the wishes of the company's board of directors (who insisted the company was doing enough).[2] BlackRock, the largest asset management firm on the planet, supported the resolution.

You may be asking yourself if these examples really matter to most individuals, to small businesses, or to employees of companies that aren't necessarily making headlines as contributors to the potential destruction of the planet. After all, we're not all in a position to be activist investors, with the shareholder power to drive big companies to behave in more sustainable ways.

Except that, in more and more cases, we are.

Almost all of us are investors in some way, whether actively in the market, or through index fund investments parked in our retirement accounts, or via the actions of the people running our pension plans. And investors in our economic system hold a lot of power. As a society, we give many decision rights to the people who invest capital into our system. Investors elect the boards of directors of public companies, who have massive impact on how those companies behave in the world. Investors have the right to the residual earnings of companies, and the legal right to compel companies to act on their behalf. If acting with an eye toward sustainability has become in large part a critical way for a company to thrive over the long run—which I hope I've effectively demonstrated is the case—then investors have the right and the responsibility to push companies in that direction.

As we have seen with ExxonMobil, Procter & Gamble, and other examples, they are absolutely doing so. Somehow, we have gone from a world that basically didn't care about these issues a decade ago—in the case of ExxonMobil, maybe not even last year—to one where many players on Wall Street and beyond understand the importance of ESG factors and are focused and engaged on these issues.

I look at initiatives like Climate Action 100+, an investor-led push started in 2017 to force the largest emitters of greenhouse gases to take action regarding climate change.[3] Some of the largest investors in the world—with more than $52 trillion in assets under management—have banded together publicly to advocate for change in 167 large companies responsible for 80 percent of greenhouse gas emissions, from Airbus to BP to The Coca-Cola Company, and from automobile manufacturers to mining companies and others. They count among their successes so far more than a dozen commitments from companies to set specific and aggressive emissions targets.

On a macro level, investors recognize that these issues matter—big institutional investors need to make sure that there is still a world to invest in a hundred years from now—and on a micro level, as we've seen, of course they do as well.

In this chapter, I explain how we have gotten to the point where investors care so deeply about these issues. I also discuss how investors of all sizes ought to think about the interaction between ESG and financial performance, and show how even the largest players are demonstrating their commitment to better ESG performance from the companies they back. Finally, I talk about what we can all do to keep the investment world focused on pushing companies in the right direction for the planet.

The newfound commitment of investors can be seen in figure 7.1, which shows the assets under management by investment

firms that have signed up to abide by the Principles for Responsible
Investment, a code of conduct that originated inside the United
Nations. From nothing when the principles were introduced in
2005, by 2020, the assets under management by PRI signatories had
surpassed $100 trillion, covering the vast majority of all investor
assets around the world.[4]

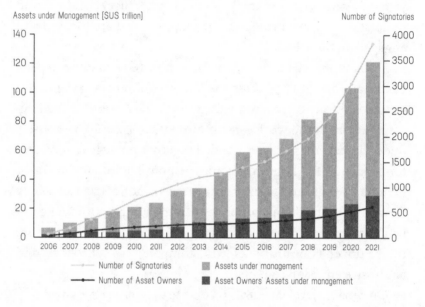

FIGURE 7.1

ESG INVESTING: IT TAKES MORE THAN
"DO-GOODERS" AND NEGATIVE SCREENING

In an article in *Barron's* in 2019, I described a conversation I had
with a former student, who was then a rising star at one of the
world's largest private equity firms. She described her struggle
getting her firm to pay attention to ESG performance in determining where to invest its money. She expected me to say that these
were issues common to every private equity firm, and that it was
a shame attitudes were still stuck in the Milton Friedman era in

this corner of the business world. However, I realized as we talked that this simply wasn't true. Her firm's reactions were entirely outside the norm. It was a wonderful feeling to realize how much the world had changed.

Her firm, unfortunately for its employees and its clients, was still stuck where so many people were in the days before data and the clear proof of alignment that data has brought us. For a long time, ESG was seen by investors as a great way to lose money, or, more delicately, as a way to perhaps give something back to the world, but not as an actual driver of economic value. When investors thought about socially responsible investing, they would invest a small slice of their portfolio in companies explicitly working on social or environmental issues, but in their minds they would write off the investment as charity, not expecting it to turn a profit or be the hero in their portfolio.

Much of this is because for decades investors lacked an understanding of what it meant to incorporate ESG issues into investor analysis. Once again, it is about transparency and data. ESG investing started out very simply with something known as negative screening—eliminating tobacco and alcohol companies from portfolios, or keeping out firms involved in scandals. At first glance it seems that negative screening is a good first step toward moving companies in a positive direction—why should a business leader risk having the company screened out by potential investors?—but it is not clear that negative screening ultimately has any positive impact, and, for several reasons, it may well have done more harm than good.

First, the only way to power real change from negative screening is if enough players in the market commit to it, so that the cost of capital for a screened-out company increases significantly. If you make doing business more costly for a particular company by creating financing problems and depressing its valuation, then theoretically it should influence its behavior. Unfortunately, at some point, the value of the company goes low enough that a private market buyer unconcerned with anything beyond making a profit may very well step in. Being screened out doesn't matter at that point, because the company is no longer looking for financing.

The entire rationale behind private equity is to buy up undervalued public companies. If negative screening were to truly have an impact on companies, the logical result might well be to shift these companies from publicly held to privately held, making their actions even less transparent and diminishing the ability of anyone to improve their behavior, short of governmental regulation. Certainly, this could not be seen as a good outcome or a reason to advocate for negative screening by investors.

Second, because negative screening as a concept was driven not by financial concerns but by social ones, it tainted the entire ESG enterprise as a chase for something other than economic performance. The assumption was that if you were paying attention to these issues, you were driven by personal values and not financial performance, and that you might even be at risk of violating your fiduciary duties as an investment manager. One of my early papers on this subject (written with Professor Ioannis Ioannou) looked at two decades of Wall Street analyst recommendations.[5] Our research showed that, in the 1990s, industry experts were in fact issuing more pessimistic buy-sell-hold recommendations for companies with strong sustainability performance than would be otherwise expected. Companies motivated to act in socially beneficial ways were not just being ignored. They were actively penalized. The old-style thinking was that if you were a high-performing ESG company, you must be focused on something other than profits, and, therefore, experts did not expect you to outperform in the future.

Over the course of time, as figure 7.2 indicates, this trend slowly reversed, and the recommendations became less pessimistic at first, and, finally, turned around and became more positive for firms with high corporate social responsibility scores. The bias went away, and the investment world began to realize that it wasn't just that these efforts were not destroying value in companies, but, in fact, ESG efforts were going hand in hand with increased performance. Analysts were seeing the same data as companies were: ESG efforts could be important and meaningful from a strategic perspective.

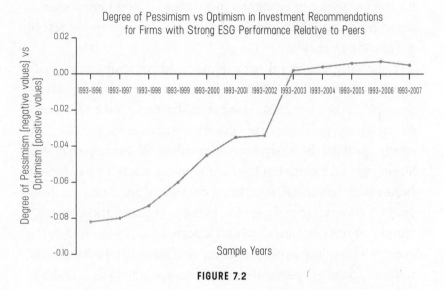

FIGURE 7.2

My research indicates that as the data got better the stigma faded, and investors—starting with more experienced analysts, and trickling down to the rest of the industry—realized that ESG issues are absolutely strategic levers. From there, it was only a short leap for investors to start actively engaging with initiatives like Climate 100+ and the kinds of shareholder resolutions passed by ExxonMobil and Procter & Gamble.

A NEW KIND OF BARGAIN HUNTING: UNRECOGNIZED ESG VALUE

Of course, it isn't as easy as that story makes it sound. It rarely is. We know by now that ESG performance isn't a magic bullet, and just as it doesn't always pay off for companies, deciding to factor it into investment decisions doesn't automatically make a portfolio a winner. Just as with any investment, it all comes down to value. If the price is too high, no matter how much a company is committed to saving the forests, lowering carbon emissions, paying its workers fairly, or eliminating child labor in its supply chain, it's still not going to be a great investment. A good investment is about predicting the future, and finding value before the rest of the market catches up.

Following the trend of buy-sell-hold recommendations, I found similar results around investment pricing over the past two decades.[6] In the early 2000s, companies that had good environmental, social, and governance performance traded at a slight discount, consistent with the analyst recommendations showing that Wall Street viewed strong ESG performance as costly to a company rather than beneficial. Analyzing data on more than two thousand US companies and a similar number of international firms, I found that this discount slowly disappeared and, by the mid-2010s, became a premium as people started to realize that, looking to the future, strong ESG performers would do better than their underlying numbers predicted.

As you can see in figure 7.3, this premium completely collapsed as soon as Donald Trump was elected president of the United States in late 2016. Investors feared that the regulatory environment would change, and that being a strong ESG performer would be far less meaningful in a world where the incentives may not support those kinds of behaviors. Yet, the power of the new alignment proved stronger than politics. By early 2017, the premium completely recovered.

We have been able to use artificial intelligence to measure public sentiment around different companies, and here's where the research gets particularly surprising. We found that if you look at companies with equally strong ESG performance—the ones that are already viewed favorably by the public, with high public sentiment scores—they don't outperform expectations. They already trade at

FIGURE 7.3

appropriate multiples, and their ESG performance is baked into the price. On the other hand, companies that don't yet have high public sentiment scores, but still have strong ESG strategies and performance, outperform in the future. This tracks the results of NextEra and AES. Companies like AES, not yet recognized for their strong ESG performance, are bargains; they are the ones with untapped potential, and the ones for which there is still value to be recognized.

If you are an investor, this is what you're looking for—the unheralded performers who will soon be noticed. Even better, if you can find a company that isn't yet maximizing its ESG potential, and you can become an activist investor that helps push it there—like the ExxonMobil investors!—then you can get in on the ground floor and reap all of the rewards of outperformance as the world realizes the strategic opportunity at hand and pushes the company's price toward an ESG-fueled premium. This actually is the whole point of active investing—to uncover hidden opportunities. Thus, this potential to capture untapped value is now driving even the most traditionally conservative and profit-focused players to turn significant attention to sustainability.

This kind of thinking drew me to join the advisory board of Inherent Group, an activist hedge fund, founded by the successful investor Tony Davis, who believed that businesses that incorporate sustainability factors into their strategy and operations would outperform the competition. We think of hedge funds as the most money-focused investment vehicles out there, traditionally run by the people we would think would be the last to accept the idea that "soft" factors are worth considering. Tony experienced wild success early in his career, which allowed him to retire in his midforties, but he returned to the industry to start Inherent. As he explained to me in 2018, he felt the chance to deploy his investment skills to help companies execute meaningful change on environmental and social issues was the opportunity of a century.

On the one hand, Inherent looks for companies with potential to increase their value through better ESG performance, and then invests and engages with management, putting pressure on them to execute. On the other hand, when they see companies on the wrong side of sustainability trends, Inherent short-sells, looking to profit in the future as the stock price plummets as company misalignment becomes a liability. It's a way to benefit on both sides of the new reality.

SUSTAINABILITY: THE NEXT GENERATION

David Blood is the cofounder (with former vice president Al Gore) and senior partner of Generation Investment Management, one of the first investment firms to fully integrate sustainability analysis into their decision-making and declare their focus on long-term sustainable performance. The firm started in 2004 with $400 million under management and now has close to $30 billion—and by 2020 topped rankings as the highest-performing fund (out of 169 global equity funds) over the past twelve years. Having worked for years with Generation on the importance of sustainability factors in long-term investment decisions, its success does not surprise me.

When I think about the journey that Generation has taken over the past decade and a half, I remember a presentation I gave in Los Angeles almost ten years ago to asset allocators and managers of family offices and other relatively small funds. It was a hostile crowd, filled with people who were still very skeptical about the importance of ESG investing, convinced that they would be sacrificing returns, and having a lot of trouble believing my data. At the end of my talk, one audience member told me that he had been a skeptic, but Generation changed his thinking. He had invested in the fund without any expectations, putting the investment in a separate bucket from the rest of his choices, figuring that maybe he could do some good but never believing it would actually be a profitable choice. Then it outperformed all of his mainstream investments, and his biggest wish was that he had invested even more money with them. His expectations were completely misaligned with what actually happened.

You may recall Reynir Indahl, and his firm, Summa Equity, a private equity firm focused on ESG issues with more than $1 billion invested. Reynir explained to my HBS class the challenge but also the reward of embedding sustainability considerations into every decision his firm makes. Because they are known as an investor that does things differently, Summa is able at times to buy companies even when it is not the highest bidder. Summa is viewed by entrepreneurs as a credible partner in maintaining and strengthening the company's purpose, and able to add value beyond what other potential investors can.

I can point to many other examples beyond these two. I started working with John Streur in 2015 when he became CEO of Calvert Research and Management, an investment firm that focuses on responsible and sustainable investing. Calvert was one of the first firms to create socially responsible investment products. Even after more than thirty years in the field, Calvert still faced resistance when making its case to portfolio managers. There wasn't enough understanding of the data, and clients were leaving to go elsewhere, unconvinced that Calvert's mission aligned with smart, financially sound investing. The firm lost hundreds of millions of dollars in assets under management over just a few short years. John and I dove deeper in an effort to understand what elements were driving sustainable companies to success (specifically, materiality and the importance of robust data), and clients were finally able to embrace the vision. John turned it around. He almost tripled the firm's assets under management to more than $30 billion by 2020, and is reaping the rewards of smart, research-backed sustainable investments.

A couple more:

The Carlyle Group—one of the largest private equity firms in the world—credits sustainability as a huge difference-maker. "As stewards of our investors' capital," they wrote in 2018, "Carlyle's mandate is to invest wisely and create value. Over the last decade, one of the ways we have strengthened our stewardship is through our sustainability practice: quite simply, sound ESG practices enhance our investment processes and outcomes."[7]

Morgan Stanley launched the Institute for Sustainable Investing in 2013 with a goal of raising $10 billion for sustainable and impact investing within five years. They far exceeded the goal and now have $25 billion in client assets under management. Audrey Choi, Morgan Stanley's chief sustainability officer, told an audience of 350 during a conference I organized that nobody had expected such growth, and that many were initially quite skeptical about the institute.[8] They have been proven wrong.

This is not to say everyone is doing business this way. In fact, Reynir Indahl often talks about the greenwashing that many private equity firms' marketing materials engage in. They say the right things but do not necessarily back them up with action. He believes that Summa's competitive advantage plays out because people are now seeing through the greenwashing and recognizing that what his firm does is different; he is truly pushing companies to improve in ways that not only help the world but also reduce risk and enhance returns, disrupt industries, improve supply chains, and more. The trend lines are clear. Even if not everyone is as wholeheartedly committed as Reynir Indahl, David Blood, John Streur, and others, at this point it's far easier to ask who doesn't think it's important to consider sustainability when investing than to ask who does.

Who is not yet on board, and why not? That is not a rhetorical question; it is actually really important to ask. To some extent, those left behind are people still stuck in the old paradigm, believing ESG investing still means negative screening. They are not looking at the research my colleagues and I have been doing over the past decade, and they are not looking at their peers and understanding why industry behavior has changed. There are people who have succeeded over time and have ignored ESG factors, who don't feel the need to adjust. That's not to say that incorporating these factors would not improve their performance; it almost certainly would, but success breeds overconfidence, and creates inertia that encourages people to stick with what they have always done. Every empire declines eventually, and every smart investment strategy loses its effectiveness over time as knowledge moves forward and the industry adopts the ideas of the leaders. Those who don't embrace the new alignment will be left behind if they haven't been already; it's as simple as that.

THE BOTTOM LINE: INNOVATING FOR ACCOUNTABILITY

Having come this far, I believe you can see that the sustainable investing movement is now victorious. It feels like such a different landscape than it did just a few years ago. Today, so many investors are acting in ways that demonstrate an understanding of the power of alignment, and reflect their deep care and concern for society. Even more powerful is that we have begun to see innovations in the financial markets that don't just rely on investors believing the research, but actually link ESG outcomes to the bottom line in extraordinarily meaningful ways.

In September 2020, the global pharmaceutical company Novartis announced the first sustainability-linked bond in the health care industry. I mentioned sustainability bonds earlier, and Google's bond specifically, committing the company to invest in sustainability and demonstrating to employees that the company truly cares about these issues. Novartis's bond commits the company to pay bondholders a higher rate of interest if it can't meet a set of Patient Access Targets by 2025. These targets have to do with the global availability of medicines for diseases like malaria and leprosy that are ravaging the developing world. The bond, reads Novartis's press release, "represents another bold step in the company's journey to further embed ESG into the core of its business operations and to communicate progress in a consistent and transparent way."[9]

The Italian electricity and gas company Enel issued a similar sustainability-linked bond in 2020, increasing the interest rate by twenty-five basis points if sustainability targets are not achieved.[10] These kinds of bonds and other sustainability loan instruments put strong financial incentives on good behavior and allow a company to put real teeth behind their promises and commitments. Three years ago, they didn't exist; now, as of this writing, hundreds of billions of dollars have been issued using these types of instruments. It is extraordinary to see sustainability outcomes linked so literally to the bottom line, forcing companies to do the right thing if they want cheaper money, and making them internalize the outcomes of their behavior.

In some ways, it all comes back to negative screening—but not yesterday's negative screening. Now, we can negatively screen in far more meaningful ways. With sustainability-linked instruments, it becomes easy to screen out companies that have not met their targets, because their profits are clearly impacted by their failure to act sustainably. I was one of six members of New York's first-ever decarbonization advisory panel, appointed by the governor of New York and the comptroller of New York State's common retirement fund, which has $220 billion under management. Our objective was to decide how to protect the pension fund from the financial risks of climate change.

Instead of making a simple decision to divest—a popular political strategy and one about which every member of the committee received many emails from advocates—the fund decided to follow our recommendation to adopt a multi-pronged approach. It set minimum standards for every company about the outcomes it needed to reach in order for the fund to remain invested, and committed the fund to divest if the company did not meet those goals. The fund also injected billions of dollars into investments that would actively provide climate solutions. It was a tremendous example of putting data into practice and making the risks of poor ESG performance clear: if you wanted the New York State retirement fund to continue to invest in your company, you needed to act with the planet in mind.[11]

These issues matter to pension funds, maybe more than to most players because they know they have long time horizons and need the world to be in good enough shape a hundred years from now to be able to pay out their obligations. This is why investing in fossil fuels is so dangerous for pension funds. If that business goes away—due to regulation, or the forced internalization of the climate change risks those companies create—then those investments may potentially go to zero. Divestment as a general policy is not a perfect answer, but it does indicate that people are paying more attention and care deeply about these issues.

Hiro Mizuno, the former chief investment officer of the $1.6 trillion Japanese Global Pension Investment Fund and now a board member of Tesla, is a regular guest speaker at my Harvard Business School classes. He explains that managing a pension fund means thinking in hundred-year terms, and not about the next quarter or year. GPIF owns more than 1 percent of almost every large publicly listed company in the world (and more than 5 percent of almost all large Japanese companies), so Mizuno had tremendous power to influence business leaders. A few years ago, he had a stunning insight that changed the way we should all think about the power of the largest investors: A manager could work to find the right investments to make the portfolio just a little bit better than average, he realized, and certainly no one would complain. Alternatively, the same manager could realize that a fund was so big, and invested in almost everything, that it wasn't much of a victory to only lose 9 percent if the market dropped 10 percent. Rather than being content with a small out-performance in a down market, couldn't the manager do something instead to keep the market from losing that 10 percent in the first place?

Hiro explains to my classes that he started questioning the traditional evaluation model of the asset manager. Instead of just trying to beat the market, he and his team came up with the concept of universal ownership. "We own the universe, so we cannot beat the universe." Instead, he spent his time on trying to make the universe more sustainable.

Hiro decided that instead of just making his portfolio better, he would make the world better. "One pension fund manager told me, 'Our job is to save money, not save the planet,'" Hiro told my class in the spring of 2021. "Someone else told me that I sound like a religious leader, not a financial expert. They told me I was violating my fiduciary duty. People tried to push back with every possible reason, but I asked them, 'What is the point of getting your full pension if our children can't even play outside?'"

Hiro is bold in his thinking, and it is not as if everyone has immediately seen the light. However, his story illustrates just how much power and influence large investors can have in changing the world. Of course, we are not all Hiro Mizuno, and we are not all in charge of enormous pension funds. But that just brings us full circle back to the question at the start of this chapter: What can we do as individuals to help promote these types of efforts?

Certainly, you can pressure the asset managers you invest with, and, as I found in my work with New York State, it really can make a difference. In the United Kingdom, there is something even more public, for everyone to take part in. Make My Money Matter is a new initiative where citizens can look up their pensions and find out where their money is invested.[12] "There's about £3 trillion invested in UK pensions," announces the website. "Lots of it funds harmful industries like fossil fuels, tobacco, and arms. We're here to demand it does better, through investments that do good not harm, and by using our pension power to ensure the companies we invest in do the same." Transparency is the first step. We can all demand better behavior.

PRISONERS NO LONGER

If we step back and look at the big picture, it becomes clear: companies need to do their best. However, not all companies live up to that goal. What if an ESG issue does not increase returns and you have companies that are willing to do social damage in pursuit of profit? After all, while the evidence suggests that, in general, firms with better ESG performance outperform their competitors, there are cases where this will not be true. As one example, there is the "customer does not want to pay" problem: in some cases, consumers are simply not willing to pay more for "green" products, and in many cases it is only a small subset of the customer base that is even interested in choosing a greener product, price considerations aside. As a result, firms that take costly actions to source products in sustainable ways can find themselves with higher cost structures and lower profitability margins—a significant competitive disadvantage.

Another set of problems emerges from the issue of time horizons. While in some cases increasing wages or selecting suppliers with better labor practices might yield financial benefits in the long run, short-term pressures on businesses might make leaders averse to such investments. The short-term-focused design of executive compensation packages and the board of directors' evaluation horizons could be significant barriers to such decisions.

Welcome to a classic prisoner's dilemma.

If every company is forced to act responsibly, we are all better off and no one company pays a competitive price. Still, each company has its own incentive to defect, and reap the benefits. If one company defects, it alone reaps financial reward, and the planet is still mostly protected. If they all follow that logic, then they will all defect, and contribute to collective disaster. Incentives that force them to cooperate—to make them behave for their own good—become necessary.

While a challenge, finding the right incentives is not always impossible. One answer is what I call "precompetitive collaborations," where an industry comes together to cooperatively develop standards, generate data, create knowledge, or fuel product development. We already observe them in several industries, from mining to technology. They differ from collusion (the harmful practice of secretly cooperating in order to keep prices high or competitors from entering the market) in that these collaborations are transparent and beneficial.

For instance, denim industry leaders in Amsterdam, with the help of the Amsterdam University of Applied Sciences, have formed the Alliance for Responsible Denim (ARD), which helps member companies produce denim in a more sustainable way, minimizing chemicals and the damage to water and energy sources. Another example is the trade organization for mobile phone operators, which developed a framework to help its members achieve a set of goals around improving infrastructure, reducing poverty, providing quality education, and limiting damage to the climate. The International Council on Mining and Metals developed transparency principles for mining firms. The Global Agribusiness Alliance is helping to produce standards of conduct for improving the livelihoods of farmers.

The firms that have banded together in these ways—and there are many more examples in a wide range of industries—are changing norms and expectations. This makes it far harder for other companies to act irresponsibly. There is no legal force, but there is transparency, and often that is enough to keep companies from deviating. By banding together, setting standards, and releasing data, firms in a particular industry can make life much harder for free riders who seek to act less responsibly. These collaborations help to show the market which firms are committed to ESG efforts and who is shirking responsibility.

There is an important role for investors here. In my research, I have identified and laid out a framework for how investors can help build and sustain these kinds of collaborations, and I have already seen progress.[13] For example, Sweden's national pension funds, in collaboration with other investors in 2016, helped bring together ten companies to better manage the supply chains for fish and shellfish, and worked with several other companies to act more sustainably in their purchasing of cobalt mines in the Congo. In 2018, the Norwegian pension fund (the world's largest) partnered with UNICEF to help top fashion companies improve children's rights throughout their supply chains, providing access to education and better health and nutrition.

In figure 7.4, we can see a decomposition of ESG issues based on whether or not an individual firm-level action is value-enhancing. In the upper node, we see the value of collaboration where stewardship of the environment is consistent with the stewardship of investor assets.

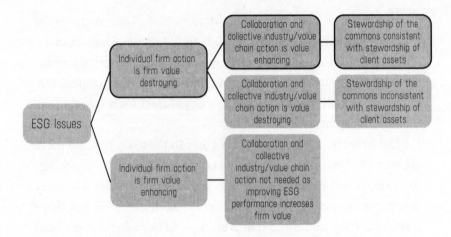

FIGURE 7.4

The reality is that all of us have broad interest as pensioners in the well-being of both the environment and society. We are invested in broadly diversified portfolios and we will hold them for a very long time. If you are in your thirties, you are looking at a fifty-year investment horizon. We are not alone there. Many institutions exhibit both large investment breadth and long holding horizons, as illustrated in figure 7.5.

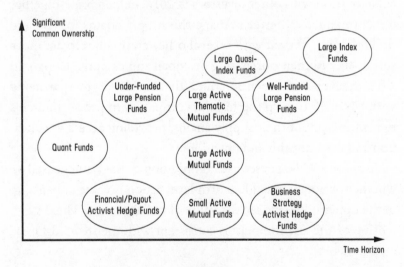

FIGURE 7.5

This is why funds that exhibit these characteristics, such as pension funds or large index managers, are so important when it comes to sustainability. They are positioned to be "stewards of the commons" across many issues and industries. For instance, as seen in figure 7.6 on page 144, the big three index asset managers (BlackRock, Vanguard, State Street) hold significant positions across industries facing a number of significant threats, such as bribery and corruption in the construction industry, deforestation in the food products space, or water pollution in the apparel business. The figure shows the average, median, and first and third quartile percentage of shares owned by large index funds across companies operating in those specific industries. As investors, we need to ensure that we hold these asset managers accountable for the power they have in affecting the behavior of the companies they invest in.

One survey has found that almost three-quarters of investors are interested in sustainable investing, and that millennials are twice as likely as the general investor population to target ESG funds specifically. More and more pension funds and family offices are demanding that ESG issues be incorporated into investment decisions, and a substantial minority go as far as to require it in their contracts.

INDEXING FOR ESG SUCCESS

As a result of these growing investor preferences, we are seeing the kind of behavior from asset managers that we might predict. In 2017, Ron O'Hanley, then CEO of State Street Global Advisors, decided to make a bold move. SSGA realized that, through its index funds, it was a permanent shareholder in many companies that had no women on their boards of directors. This struck O'Hanley as wrong, and something worth acting on. The organization rallied around the cause of diversity in the boardroom, motivated by a deeply held belief that gender diversity (and, as a result, diversity

| Topic | Industry | Year | Percent of Shares Held by Large Index Funds | | | |
			Average	Median	1st Quartile	3rd Quartile
Bribery and Corruption	Building Construction General Contractors and Operative Builders	2002	5.6	5.3	4.3	8.2
		2007	11.8	11.4	8.6	11.7
		2012	14.4	14.5	14.5	15.9
		2016	19.7	20.3	20.1	20.3
Deforestation	Food and Kindred Products	2002	5.8	6.6	1.7	8.3
		2007	8	8.6	1.8	11.8
		2012	13.5	14.1	13.3	15.9
		2016	16.5	15.9	15.9	17.4
Water Pollutants and Water Consumption	Apparel and Other Finished Products Made from Fabrics and Similar Materials	2002	5	6.7	2.3	7.6
		2007	8.1	9	5.6	10.1
		2012	10.2	8.9	8.6	12.1
		2016	13	13.3	13.2	13.4
Materials Sourcing and Conflict Minerals	Electronic and Other Electrical Equipment and Components, except Computer Equipment	2002	7.4	8.1	7.1	8.5
		2007	10.4	10.4	9.2	12.6
		2012	13.1	13.7	13.5	13.9
		2016	16.9	17	16.7	18.2
Obesity and Customer Health	Eating and Drinking Places	2002	8.1	9	6.9	10.3
		2007	10.5	10.9	9.5	11.7
		2012	13.9	14.5	13	15
		2016	17.5	18.1	15.6	19
Inclusion, Access to Affordable Products	Educational Services	2002	5	5.3	4.5	5.3
		2007	9.1	9	8.6	11
		2012	14.4	15.7	13.4	16.5
		2016	13.2	12.7	12.7	17.7

FIGURE 7.6

of thought and experience) is good governance and good business. To help break the glass ceiling at these companies, SSGA launched the Fearless Girl Campaign, placing a statue of a fearless girl at Wall Street itself. A firm that people traditionally thought of as a passive investor suddenly became an active one.

SSGA wrote letters to company leadership explaining why they should take action on behalf of diverse boards of directors. SSGA would vote against directors at future annual meetings if no change was implemented. As a result, a shift happened. In 2021, 862 companies of the 1,486 companies SSGA identified as having all-male boards (approximately 58 percent) added at least one female director.[14] As a symbol of this success, SSGA installed a broken glass ceiling around its fearless girl statue.

Helping to bring more industries and companies on board to care deeply about ESG issues is a worthwhile endeavor for virtually all investors. Holding a diversified collection of stocks for the long term means that investors are exposed to the risks of the broader economy, and not just the particular risks of one company. Whatever might put the brakes on broad economic growth—corruption, inequality of opportunity, climate change—will negatively affect assets. Across the entire economy, it becomes very difficult to hedge against systemic risks.

None of this means that all we can do is buy index funds and hope that large asset managers do the work of convincing companies how important ESG performance is to their future. There are now many socially responsible investment funds—and organizations, such as Ceres, a sustainability nonprofit that works with investors and companies to advocate for change—that put real pressure both on companies and larger investors to act responsibly. The more individual investors show that they care about the environmental and social attributes of their investments, the less likely it is that asset managers will ignore these factors.

My research shows that as individual investor interest in ESG performance has grown, we have absolutely seen an increase in the

number of asset managers engaging with companies and trying
to push them to do more and do better. Asset managers are seeing their engagement efforts as a critical part of the service that
they provide. In a world where investment services are being com-
moditized, engagement is seen as a real differentiator. We are not
powerless, and big investors are *certainly* not powerless.

ESG AND YOU: IT'S PERSONAL

Our roles as investors, as important as they can be, are usually at a
distance. Even the roles that some of us may play leading companies and making the kinds of decisions I've covered can be limited
in time or in scope. Some students tell me they don't plan on ever
running a company, or running an investment fund, and ask if these
issues really matter in their lives. My answer is that of course they
do. I started this book talking about the purpose of business and
the reasons we pursue it as a career. That is where I want to close
it. The issue of why we do what we do percolates every decision
we make. We all strive for meaning in our lives and in our careers.

As we make choices about our paths in life, we inevitably think
about whether we are working to make the world a better place. In
the final chapter, I will look at how these issues affect each of us in
our careers, and how we can approach our professional lives, fully
informed by the intersection of purpose and profit. How can each
of us make the biggest impact, choose the right opportunities, and
find the most fulfilling journey for ourselves?

Chapter Eight

ALIGNMENT: NOW OR LATER?

Not long ago, a former student asked my advice about a business decision. He had experienced a significant amount of career success in the handful of years since graduating from Harvard Business School. He was leading a business unit for a large industrial company, and reasonably satisfied with his work, but looking for a new challenge. He had been approached by an energy company, one with a somewhat spotty record of environmental stewardship, that was looking for someone to lead a much larger department. It would be a step up, and he would have normally been excited about taking it, but he was deeply passionate about the environment and committed to working on behalf of the planet, not against it.

"I know what you're going to say," he told me, "but I want to ask you anyway. Should I take the job?"

To his surprise, I immediately said, "Yes."

ALIGNED OR MISALIGNED: CHOOSING TO DRIVE CHANGE

My answer might confuse you, just as it confused him at first. Why would I advise that someone go and work for an organization that is misaligned with one of the biggest issues facing society? Why—after chapter upon chapter explaining why it's not just important to be on the right side of these matters, but that it's far better business strategy—would I encourage someone to take a step like this?

The reason is that alignment is not static. Alignment changes over the course of months and years, and it's not always entirely out of our control. We all have the power to push organizations in different directions. The questions become about figuring out how to exert our influence to make an organization do better, and about the kind of experience we want to have in our careers.

We all need to engage in thoughtful reflection about what gives us fulfillment in our professional lives, and what will feel most satisfying over time. On the one hand, there are people who choose to work at a place that is very strongly aligned with their values—say, a nonprofit focused on an issue they are passionate about—but over time, that alignment may not grow, and might even fall a bit as they and the organization change.

On the other hand, there are others who choose to work somewhere that may at first be less aligned with their goals—like my student—but, over time, they can push that company toward better performance along all kinds of dimensions, and significantly improve that alignment.

There may well be higher psychological reward, and in fact more good done for the planet, if you can help influence an organization to get better than if you work somewhere that doesn't need your help growing or maintaining its ethical performance. In fact, my intuition says that the world is better off if skilled, passionate business leaders join misaligned organizations (ones with a plausible path for improvement) rather than ones already behaving in this way.

To that end, I ask my students what matters more to them, the level of alignment they have now, or the slope of that line over time. Figure 8.1 illustrates this question. Imagine an organization that has a high level of alignment, but that alignment does not grow over time, and might even decline. This is what the top line of the figure represents. Compare this option to working in an organization that starts out with a much lower level of alignment, but because of your efforts and those of your colleagues, over time it grows. This is what the two middle lines represent.

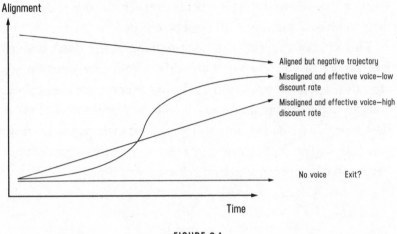

FIGURE 8.1

Where the two differ is in the speed at which they change. In one case, there will be many years with little progress, but then there is exponential improvement. In the other case, improvement is faster but linear, with a lower amount of total progress in the end. The difference between the two comes down to patience, or what I label as your own personal discount rate.

The line at the bottom is the situation you want to avoid, where there is a low level of alignment to start, and little improvement over the course of time. Here the most effective option is likely an exit from the company. I have seen people choose any of the top three lines, with the choice coming down to personal preference. Some people prioritize the level of the initial alignment (for example, wanting to work for a company that provides organic food or access to health care for underserved populations) with little concern about whether it grows over time. Others prefer to see their efforts and experience have a meaningful impact on the organization's sustainability trajectory.

It becomes about choosing among three parameters: the lowest level of alignment you are willing to accept, the desired future growth in the alignment, and the speed of that growth. (In mathematics, those second and third parameters are the first and second derivatives of alignment with respect to time.)

This kind of thinking can liberate people. You don't have to feel trapped by your choices if you think about your situation not just at the moment you begin a role, but over the course of time. You can change an organization—or you can leave. You can look at the trajectory instead of only worrying about where you are now. You may well prefer beginning in a situation of misalignment but having an effective voice to bring change over time.

YOU DON'T NEED TO BE A CEO

People are often tempted to push back. You can't change an organization, they say, unless you are at the top. Not so. Research—mine and my colleagues'—shows that you actually don't need to be a CEO in order to make the kinds of changes you might envision.[1] Just as in our research about corporate purpose, where the attitudes of middle managers drove the association between higher performance and being a purposeful organization, there may be hugely important roles here for people who are not necessarily at the top of the company.

The story of another former student illustrates this. Jonathan Bailey joined McKinsey & Company, the global consulting powerhouse, back in 2012. McKinsey has had a huge impact advising companies and governments all around the world. In fact, in the 2020 Democratic presidential primary race, Pete Buttigieg drew criticism from his rivals for his time working at McKinsey precisely because the firm works with so many big players, many of whom aren't necessarily known for doing the right thing.

Jonathan started out as an associate and worked his way up to director and eventually junior partner. Even before he made it to the partner level, he was instrumental in designing and operation-alizing a new program—a quite significant one—that McKinsey launched with the Canadian Pension Plan Investment Board on the importance of long-termism in tackling issues such as climate change, good jobs, and sound corporate governance. That work became the starting point for an even larger initiative: a new non-profit organization, Focusing Capital on the Long-Term, which has some of the largest companies and investors in the world advo-cating for the need for business to adopt an orientation far more focused on the long term.

These programs wouldn't have launched without leadership commitment from senior partners, including then-managing part-ner Dominic Barton and senior partner Conor Kehoe, but the careful work and due diligence from people like Jonathan Bailey made it happen.

LEADERSHIP MATTERS AT EVERY LEVEL

Being an effective leader—at any level of an organization—means understanding what you are trying to achieve, and then figuring out how to motivate the right behavior to make it happen. Some people think that with passion and emotion, they can make the biggest difference, but I believe we are far more effective when we can point to the concrete goals we are trying to reach, and then master all the skills we need to reach them.

Paul Polman at Unilever didn't just move the company toward sustainability because he believed in it; he moved the company because he was an amazingly effective leader who knew the busi-ness inside and out. He mastered the numbers, he had complete clarity about what actions would lead to what consequences, and he could pull the right levers to get to the destination he hoped for.

Any significant change will take time. The work is incremental and sometimes slow, but incremental progress is still progress. If an organization is striving for 50 percent diversity, and is only at 10 percent now, just because you can't immediately get all the way to 50 percent isn't a reason to throw your hands in the air and give up. You can get to 12 percent, then 14 percent, then 16 percent, and onward from there. Small amounts of progress matter.

THE RIGHT INGREDIENTS FOR SUCCESS

This is not necessarily as straightforward as I might be making it sound. Our efforts don't always pan out. There is risk—ranging from the very simple risk that you aren't able to move your organization and it remains misaligned to the risk that it all blows up in scandal, and you and the organization are both irreparably damaged. At the very least, resistance and frustration will likely be in your future, at least at the beginning, if you take on the challenge of helping a company transform itself.

We can return to the story of Erik Osmundsen. We talked in chapter five about his personal challenges cleaning up Norsk Gjenvinning, the largest waste management company in Norway. There is more to learn from his story as it relates to what exactly a leader who is focused on creating alignment can do. Osmundsen's efforts spanned the company, changing the culture from "this is the way it has always been done" to a new atmosphere of responsibility and values.[2]

Erik began by hiring leaders from outside the waste industry, who would not be steeped in the corrupt practices common to NG's competitors. He tried to attract the most talented people that he could: diverse, technically gifted, and committed to the same values Erik was trying to institute in his company. He was transparent with the media; he told them that there would be new discoveries of bad behavior. He knew there were skeletons in the closet and trusted that eventually they would be found, but declaring that up front and committing not to hide things made people trust him. Erik emphasizes that employees now say, "For the first time I feel like this company is something I trust and can be proud of."[3]

After three years—with a negative business impact at first, losing 150 million Norwegian kroner in cash, and having customers stolen away by ex-employees—the company is now stronger than before, and is leading the industry from both an ethical perspective and an economic one. It has become the eleventh most reputable company in Norway, and number one in terms of work environment. It has become more than just a supplier to its customers, but a strategic partner, helping them become more sustainable themselves, giving them recycled materials, and taking them on the same sustainability journey Erik put his own company through.

Being different from the competition enabled the company to distinguish itself, to stand out, and to make its reform efforts something worth talking about in the media. These efforts have been a huge driver of new business, strengthening margins, and increasing NG's multiple in the financial markets.

HAZARDS AND WARNING SIGNS

Erik found success, but it was by no means guaranteed. Before you jump to a misaligned organization and take on these challenges, you should understand the risks and red flags. First, you want to be in an environment that is open to change. If leaders don't recognize the need for alignment, and there is no support for your efforts to create it, you run the risk of disappointment. It is not always possible for one voice (even the CEO) to move an entire company, and it may turn out that choosing a different organization—or exiting if you are already there—is the better option.

I was once told by a thirty-five-year-old engineer at a big oil and gas firm that there was much energy and talent inside the firm, but all the senior managers had disregarded (and in fact ridiculed) ideas, developed by the incredibly talented technical workers, that emerged in the company's innovation pipeline. This created a vicious cycle where people felt disempowered and disengaged, and the most talented workers kept leaving, depriving the organization of exactly the innovation it needed to thrive. Professor Amy Edmondson, my colleague at Harvard Business School, has written extensively about this issue of psychological safety in organizations. Amy emphasizes that psychological safety isn't about being nice. It is about giving candid feedback, openly admitting mistakes, and having workers learn from each other.

This is why a strong corporate purpose is more important than ever, although its importance was first recognized a long time ago—about a century ago, by thought leaders such as Chester Barnard and Philip Selznick, who studied organizations and their role in society. In their view, purpose was as central to guiding organizations as prices were to markets.

As Barnard wrote, "Organizations endure . . . in proportion to the breadth of the morality by which they are governed. . . . Foresight, long purposes, high ideals, are the basis for the persistence of cooperation."[4] Selznick advocated a similar conception: purpose enabled companies to evolve from "expendable organizations" to "enduring institutions," infused with value and identity.[5]

WHAT WE CAN DO; WHAT WE NEED TO UNDERSTAND

The best things we can do as individuals and as leaders are work to ensure the alignment of our organizations, be proactive about spotting problems, and do our best to make the slope of our careers get us closer and closer to perfection.

Of course, our careers won't ever be perfect. We will never find or even create jobs that are in perfect alignment with our goals, and no company will ever be perfect in its behavior on the ground. As I have said throughout this book, doing all of this is hard. Balancing profits and social impact, making the right choices along the way, executing, communicating, and uncovering value are all difficult things to do well. My hope is that I have made it clear that these pathways are getting just a little bit easier, and success is being rewarded more and more in the marketplace.

In the conclusion, I talk about how we keep it all going as we move to the future, and how we continue to make sure that companies are properly incentivized to pursue social impact, held accountable for the results of their behavior, and helping to drive us toward better lives and a better planet.

THE FUTURE OF PURPOSE AND PROFIT

A couple of years ago, I spoke at a CEO-level event about how businesses can improve the state of the world. There were set to be dozens of Fortune 500 CEOs in the audience, who knew pretty much everything I was ready to tell them. They knew there was growing evidence that efforts to make a difference could pay off in the financial markets. They knew about the growing number of metrics, and the growing demands of employees, consumers, and investors. They knew the world had changed. They just did not know quite what to do about it.

The night before the event, I was invited to a private dinner, two dozen CEOs and me, having a roundtable discussion about these issues and how businesses could change their behavior to really have an impact. I remember a moment when everyone started complaining about how hard this all was. "We don't have enough data." "I want to make the investments, but I can't afford it." "I want to hire a diverse group of people, but it's impossible to find them." "I want to help the environment, but not if it means going bankrupt." "I want to change, but it's so difficult."

Finally, a CEO of a very large consumer-facing company known to everyone stood up. He held up his hand, the complaining around him stopped, and he said, very simply, "The problem isn't that we don't have the tools or the resources. The problem isn't that we don't have data. The problem is much more straightforward than that. The problem is that all of you who are complaining just don't care enough about these issues."

Everyone was silent. He went on to explain that his company had it harder than many. "We have fifty thousand suppliers. To figure out what is happening in terms of employment practices and human rights is almost impossible, but we didn't just throw up our hands and say we can't control this, so why bother. We got the data, and over the course of a few years—because, yes, it did take some time—we changed the supply chain process, with all fifty thousand suppliers."

"It happened because we cared," he continued. "It happened because we said that it's unacceptable to have human rights violations in our supply chain, unacceptable to have people coming to work every day and being mistreated, unacceptable to have people coming to work knowing about how others are being mistreated and not being able to put an end to it. It would have been easy to make lots of excuses about how difficult it was, but we didn't, because we cared."

THE UPSHOT: NAVIGATING BETWEEN VALUES AND CONFLICTING INCENTIVES

On a fundamental level, you have to care. I can give you all the tools in the world, but if you don't care enough to work to make your company, your organization, and the world a better place, I can't help you. I can give you all of the data about how changing the way you do business can have positive impacts, how it can drive investor interest, consumer interest, employee interest, and actually improve your financial performance—but to make it happen, you really do have to care.

However, caring alone is, of course, not nearly enough. Even if you care, what happens when you face a set of incentives that drives you in a fundamentally different direction? What if those incentives force you to navigate between your values and your survival as a business or the viability of your job or career? In my experience, in the vast majority of cases, incentives win.

How, then, do you keep alignment strong as you move into the future? You have to change the incentives. I talked in chapter three about impact-weighted accounts, and the importance of having a way to put numbers on behavior, to have a way to objectively understand and evaluate what a company is actually doing in the world. Many people make the mistake of thinking that is the complete answer. If we measure these impacts, will we magically solve the world's problems? No. Measurement is not the end; it is just the beginning. We need to measure—and then (and only then) can we create the right incentives to provide solutions to the environmental and social challenges facing our society.

As organizations start to measure, they are building those incentives, but we must keep in mind that we cannot take this process for granted. Alignment is fragile, and needs to be nurtured and strengthened. It is far too easy to imagine society shifting in a different direction, moving away from transparency, moving away from choice, moving away from caring enough about these issues to institute the right reforms to make change happen. Just as we cannot take democracy, or health, or access to clean air and water for granted, we cannot assume the world will keep heading in the direction we want. We have to put in the work, and we have to truly care.

THE FOUR PILLARS OF SUSTAINABLE BEHAVIOR

As we look to the future and continue to think about how we drive companies toward sustainable behavior, we need to be mindful of four pillars of sustainable behavior:

1. Continued transparency through analytics
2. Outcomes-based incentives
3. Education
4. The role of government

We will look at these one at a time.

CONTINUED TRANSPARENCY THROUGH ANALYTICS: THE EVOLVING STORY OF DANONE

I wrote earlier about Danone, the French food conglomerate known primarily in the United States as the maker of Dannon yogurt. Danone has been on the cutting edge of impact-weighted accounting. Their commitment to being purpose-driven, their drive to become carbon neutral by 2050, and their position as the first company in the world to adopt a "carbon-adjusted" earnings-per-share metric make them a leader worth admiring.

I was thrilled to write about them; yet, as I was working on this book in the spring of 2021, the company suddenly seemed to be in crisis. Chief executive Emmanuel Faber, who less than a year earlier had congratulated Danone shareholders for "toppling the statue of Milton Friedman," was forced out, a victim of unmet expectations.[1] The company was doing all the right things when it came to purpose, but it was underperforming in the capital markets. Profits were down, and despite the company's work on environmental and social issues, it was lagging behind its competitors when it came to the bottom line.

The easy way to react to this is to see it as Milton Friedman might: "I told you so, it doesn't work, impact and performance are antithetical to each other, and Danone was clearly focusing too much on one, at the expense of the other." Others might react in the opposite way: "Why are they forcing out a CEO doing such amazing work in the world? The shareholders are blind to the impact that Danone is creating."

Both sides would be acting on the same assumption, taking for granted that Danone is a great impact company. But here's the thing we have to remember: intentions are not the same as outcomes. The Danone situation would be a real setback for the ideas behind sustainable capitalism if in fact the company was achieving incredible results that simply weren't being properly valued in the marketplace. Yes, the company is a B Corp, and they have great disclosures, and terrific farming-related initiatives, wonderful policies in all sorts of different areas, but the value of impact-weighted accounting—the value of rich, accurate, objective metrics—is that we can actually look at the data and see beyond the rhetoric to what Danone is actually accomplishing.

When you look at the metrics, you realize that Danone is right in the middle in terms of actual impact among its industry peers. Not the leader, despite the transparency, and despite the good intentions. If you look at the company's carbon emissions, water consumption, the amount of generated pollutants, and all kinds of specific environmental outcomes that we want companies to excel at, Danone is underperforming peers like General Mills. If you look at Danone's products themselves, the nutrient value, the sugar and the sodium, again they are underperforming General Mills. We don't hear a lot about General Mills and its commitment to sustainability even though they are outperforming Danone. The ability to measure outcomes and not just rely on intentions and wishes is incredibly powerful. It allows you to have analytical conversations that don't devolve into ideological arguments about Milton Friedman. Maybe Danone is underperforming not in spite of its focus on impact, but because it's failing to generate *enough* impact. Maybe the CEO should have been given more time, or maybe his management team needed to change how they were implementing his goals. Maybe the purposes Danone was driving toward were absolutely the right ones, but the execution was subpar, and so replacing Faber was right—not because of his goals, but because he wasn't doing the right things to achieve them.

The right analytics get you past the sentiment, to a different and better starting point. This is why impact-weighted accounting and other metrics like it are so critical. To have sensible discussions, you need the right data, which brings us to the next pillar.

OUTCOMES-BASED INCENTIVES:
EXECUTIVE COMPENSATION AND BEYOND

In chapter five, I talked about companies like Microsoft, BHP, and Royal Shell linking executive compensation to diversity goals or carbon emissions. In chapter seven, I talked about sustainability bonds at Novartis and Enel linking interest rates to meeting certain targets. These developments are wonderful and becoming more common as time marches on. As I write this, Chipotle just announced that they will link 10 percent of executive compensation to the company's progress achieving sustainable farming and employee inclusion goals, and Canada's six largest banks are tying substantial pieces of their executive pay packages to ESG factors.[2]

This only scratches the surface of what is possible when we take a broader look at incentives and how they drive behavior. My colleague Ethan Rouen and I are the faculty cochairs of the Impact-Weighted Accounts Project at Harvard. Ethan and I recently wrote a paper about the paradigm shift that impact-weighted financial accounts could represent in the world. We take it for granted that the financial accounting system we know today is the only way to evaluate a business, but the accounting system as we know it has only become widely implemented over the past hundred years. The choice to include assets and liabilities but not impacts on the environment or on employees is exactly that: a choice. We can make a different one.

Resistance to changing our accounting standards to reflect a business's impact on the world comes in two forms. There are those who say it cannot be done, and there are those who say it should not be done. Remember, there were those who had the same resistance to what we now treat as generally accepted accounting principles. They said that every business is unique and that accounting is art rather than science. They said that financial reporting imposed too many costs on a business.

Those objections were overcome. Now, people say that broader impacts are not financially material, but, of course, as the research shared in this book makes clear, they are. Now, people say it's impossible to truly measure impact, but we are doing it, and we are doing it more comprehensively every day. The perfect cannot be the enemy of the good. Standards have gotten better and better; they will continue to do so. Some people say that not everything can, or should, be expressed in monetary terms, and that doing so may in fact hamper our progress in addressing these critical societal issues. However, not putting a price on our forests, our oceans, and our people has not led us to success in addressing these problems thus far. The climate is facing catastrophe. Population sizes of mammals, birds, fish, and reptiles have declined by 60 percent since 1970. We are failing. Why not try a different approach?

People who insist that we shouldn't measure the societal impact of business, and that this extends beyond the scope of what our accounting system should reflect, fail to understand that not measuring these impacts is just as much of a value judgment as measuring them. As Ethan and I write, "What we choose to measure reflects our values on what is important and needs to be prioritized. Allowing those impacts to remain invisible creates a perception that they are not important."

As we become better at measuring environmental and social impacts, we must incentivize businesses to value those measures. We must move to an accounting treatment that reflects the importance these measures have on our world, and push to create the right kinds of accountability structures, whether through executive compensation, interest rates on borrowing, specific contract terms, legal rules, or other standards. This will be an evolution over time, but it is important to keep moving forward and not stagnating or turning back.

EDUCATION: TRAINING THE NEXT GENERATION OF LEADERS

I often feel spoiled to be in front of a classroom of students who I believe care very much about these issues. Part of it is because of self-selection among the students who choose to take my courses. My class on reimagining capitalism, which I have taught for the past eight years with my colleague Professor Rebecca Henderson, has become hugely popular, and I don't think there are many students at Harvard or elsewhere who don't care deeply about these issues. Rebecca and I have graduated close to two thousand Harvard MBAs who have taken our class, and tens or even hundreds of thousands of students have used our materials at other universities. At last report, there were more than two thousand courses around the world built on what we are teaching at Harvard.

My colleagues and I are educating future CEOs, people who want to ultimately manage organizations and have final accountability for what companies do. We have to educate future business leaders about their agency and ability to make a difference, and the toolkits available to them to understand the impacts of their choices. If we graduate someone who doesn't understand and appreciate these issues, I believe they are at a terrible competitive disadvantage. If you are a business leader in the twenty-first century and do not know how to think intelligently about these issues, you are far less likely to be successful.

Leaders with forty-year careers ahead of them are going to have to be able to compete in 2050 and 2060, and by then we will have to be massively decarbonized. Sometimes I show my classes a video of Facebook CEO Mark Zuckerberg testifying in front of Congress about his company's missteps, and I tell them, "You do not want to be in that seat." You need to manage your business to avoid being called into Congress to defend yourself. Educators have a huge role to play in making sure students are well positioned to run ethical, sustainable, responsible companies that can succeed for all of their stakeholders.

THE ROLE OF GOVERNMENT: PROTECTOR OF THE INFORMATION ENVIRONMENT

People have very different views about the role of government. Living through the struggles of Greece in the 1980s and 1990s made me skeptical of heavy regulation and government controls. I know there are massive disagreements about how much government should be involved in controlling the activities of business, and I expect that in a hundred years we will be debating many of the same issues we are now. However, I do think that some issues cannot be ignored. Rebecca Henderson has written eloquently about the need for a carbon tax in order to avert the most negative consequences of our actions. I wholeheartedly agree, but I want to concentrate here on a different issue that we have touched on throughout the book.

It is critically important that governments protect the credibility of the information environment in which we live. Information is so fundamental to creating the alignment we are seeing between doing good for the world and being financially successful. Information enables people to act according to their true preferences, and allows them to make the choices that drive our economy. We have a challenge right now around misinformation and disinformation, around information overload and fake news and our increasing inability to reach consensus about even the most basic facts.

This is detrimental to everything I have discussed throughout this book. If I advocate for nothing else, it is that governments need to find ways to ensure the credibility of the information that is made available to investors, consumers, employees, and citizens.

The new analytics of doing good only work when these analytics are available, accurate, and understood. It's that simple.

FOR FUTURE ESG LEADERS: HOPE FOR THE FUTURE

It wasn't that long ago that I was sitting in the same seat as my students sit now, wondering what I was going to do with my life and my career, and whether I would be able to make a meaningful difference in the world. As I mentioned, one of my first jobs was analyzing and valuing insurance businesses, with no real connection to any of the topics I think about today. I was simply trying to make a living, and start my career off on the right foot.

I realized as I began to shift my work into the research that fills this book that I wanted to think bigger. I wanted to understand how people build impactful companies and positively affect the lives of others. I wanted to have agency to make choices, to exercise my voice in terms of where I was going to spend most of my waking hours, and what I was going to deliver to the world. We all want that kind of agency. We all want to use our voices to stand up for what we believe in. We all want to think that we are contributing in a useful way. That is really what this book is about. I hope I have given you the tools to understand the impacts you can make, and the impacts we are all making every day because of our choices and our actions.

As I write this, in some respects my career has come full circle, having recently joined the board of directors of a company in the very space where I started, the Liberty Mutual Group, one of the world's insurance leaders. The company gives millions of people the ability to innovate and take risks knowing that their entrepreneurial efforts and households are protected. The company reached out to me because they are committed to making progress in their business on ESG efforts, to aiming higher and doing better in terms of their impact on the world. They care, and, as I have said, caring is such a crucial first step.

I hope I have opened your eyes to the importance of environmental and social issues in business, the power we all have to make
a difference, and the care we must take to ensure the world continues on the right path. We have much more information than we've
ever had, much more opportunity to know. Now is the time when
we must convert that knowledge into action, and turn the new
analytics of purpose and profit into as much goodness for ourselves
and for the planet as we can possibly engineer. Fifty years from
now, I hope we have moved beyond any doubt that companies have
certain obligations to people and the planet, and it's all as obvious
to future leaders as the profit and loss numbers are obvious to leaders today. I hope we've effectively tackled the most pressing issues
around us, and are onto bigger and better things, new metrics, new
standards, and new expectations. And I hope that all of you will be
critical parts of that progress.

ACKNOWLEDGMENTS

This book is the product of years of hard work, not just in the writing itself but the research and thought leading up to it, and the energy spent developing the ideas within.

I have been lucky to have such tremendous support at Harvard Business School, where I studied and now teach. The former and current deans of Harvard Business School, Nitin Nohria and Srikant Datar, are two people who have been tremendous in helping me crystallize my ideas and believing in me when few people did. I still remember the day, as I was sitting in Nitin's office as an assistant professor, when he pulled out a pen and a piece of paper, drew a simple diagram, and said, "Here is what your research is all about." I still carry that diagram with me. Srikant influenced my thinking just as much when he was encouraging me to do more of the kind of work presented in this book and persist in the face of adversity, spending hours discussing with me how these ideas could be used by companies around the world.

In these pages, I have discussed my scholarly work with collaborators like Professors Ioannis Ioannou, Claudine Gartenberg, Rebecca Henderson, Robert Eccles, Paul Healy, Jody Grewal, Aaron Yoon, Mo Khan, Eddie Riedl, and Boris Groysberg. Much of the work here would have never happened without them. I met Ioannis and Claudine during our doctoral studies at Harvard. They have both been incredible friends and colleagues. Rebecca has taught me what it means to be truly open-minded, kind, and giving, welcoming me as an equal in teaching our Reimagining Capitalism course when she was a university professor at Harvard, the highest credential a member of the faculty can achieve, and I was a recently promoted associate professor. I owe her a tremendous amount of gratitude. Another person I owe much to is Robert. He is a force of nature, having moved the field of corporate reporting forward an immense amount through an unwavering determination and ability to create social change. Paul's advice and mentorship motivated me to stay in the United States and at Harvard following my doctoral years. His office door has always been open for me, and that has made a huge difference in my professional development.

My thanks also to the many colleagues who have provided feedback and suggestions throughout the year. I have had tremendous conversations with many, and a few of those discussions are worth highlighting here. Professor Krishna Palepu has been a mentor to me over the past decade. His incredible intellectual rigor and clarity have made me a better scholar. Professors Robert Kaplan, Mark Kramer, Vikram Gandhi, Ethan Rouen, Julie Battilana, Howard Koh, Peter Tufano, Colin Mayer, Amir Amel-Zadeh, Aiyesha Dey, Siko Sikochi, Dane Christensen, Venkat Kuppuswamy, Fabrizio Ferri, Ranjay Gulati, Rohit Deshpande, Michael Toffel, and Amy Edmondson have all shaped my thinking through their work, collaborations, and numerous discussions on these topics.

I must also thank the practitioners and colleagues whose work appears in the book and with whom I have collaborated at multiple points in this journey: Sir Ronald Cohen, Reynir Indahl, Jean Rogers, John Streur, and David Blood. I learned a tremendous amount from each one of them about what it means to have positive impact on the world and achieve excellence in everything one does. Special thanks to my cofounder at KKS, Sakis Kotsantonis, without whom my work would have been less fun and less fulfilling. Sakis has been not just a collaborator but a true friend and brother. Many thanks to all of the people at KKS, who have put scholarly ideas into practice creating a virtuous cycle between research and action, especially Tina Passalari, Thomas Cobti, and Niklas Pape. The same goes to the team at State Street Associates, especially Will Kinlaw, Stacie Wang, Alex Cheema-Fox, David Turkington, and Bridget Realmuto LaPerla. I also want to thank the team at the Impact-Weighted Accounts Initiative: David Freiberg, Katie Trinh, Katie Panella, Robert Zochowski, and DG Park. This team, along with Sir Ronald Cohen's vision and conviction, has allowed us to make significant progress toward impact transparency.

Thanks to Erik Osmundsen, Jarrid Tingle, Tiffany Pham, Ilham Kadri, Manuel Piñuela, Hiro Mizuno, Casey Clark, Evan Greenfield, Chris Pinney, Peter Kellner, Clara Barby, Tracy Palandjian, Jonathan Bailey, Mikkel Larsen, Sarah Williamson, Amanda Rischbieth, Tim Dunn, Tony Davis, Clarissa Hauptmann, and many more, whose stories appear in this book, or who have spoken to me and my students about these critical issues. Their actions and leadership inspire me and motivate me to reach higher. Big thanks to my friend Mike Hayes, who inspired me and encouraged me to start the process of writing this book. The same goes for my thousands of students over the years, whose career development, stories, and actions make a difference in the world every day.

Thanks to Anthony Mattero and his team at CAA, to Tim Burgard and everyone at HarperCollins Leadership for helping to make this book a reality, and to Jeremy Blachman for helping me edit this manuscript in a way that communicates the volume of research and experiences.

Thanks also for support from my good friends Dimitris Kolleris, Gabriel Karageorgiou, Dimitris Balomenos, and Efthymios Nikolopoulos. They make the world feel smaller, remaining close friends even though we live thousands of miles apart. My parents, Panagiotis and Nafsika Serafeim, have been my role models and I will be eternally grateful to them for everything that I achieve. Nothing would have been possible without their support and love. The same goes for my sister, Ioanna Serafeim, who at the most difficult moments would always drop everything immediately and make me a priority. Without my sister, I would have never taken the leap of faith moving from Greece, first to London and then eventually to Boston.

Finally, I want to thank my wife, Natalie Tejero Serafeim, and her family, Tony, Hilda, Josh, and Hildi. The moment I met Natalie, I knew I had found my other half. Natalie makes me a better person in every single way and if this book is even slightly better than you expected, it is thanks to her support, her long, objective feedback on early manuscripts, and her love.

NOTES

Introduction

1. Mozaffar Khan, George Serafeim, and Aaron Yoon, "Corporate Sustainability: First Evidence on Materiality," *Accounting Review* 91, no. 6 (November 2016), pp. 1697–1724, https://papers.ssrn.com/sol3/papers.cfm?abstract_id=2575912.
2. Alex Cheema-Fox, Bridget LaPerla, George Serafeim, and Hui (Stacie) Wang, "Corporate Resilience and Response During COVID-19," Harvard Business School Accounting & Management Unit Working Paper No. 20-108 (September 23, 2020), https://papers.ssrn.com/sol3/papers.cfm?abstract_id=3578167.

Chapter One: The Business of Being in Business: What Has Changed

1. Erik Kirschbaum, "German Automakers Who Once Laughed on Elon Musk Are Now Starting to Worry," *Los Angeles Times*, April 19, 2016, https://www.latimes.com/business/autos/la-fi-hy-0419-tesla-germany-20160419-story.html.
2. "Tesla Market Cap Surpasses Next Five Largest Automotive Companies Combined," Reuters Events, January 7, 2021, https://www.reutersevents.com/supplychain/technology/tesla-market-cap-surpasses-next-five-largest-automotive-companies-combined.
3. Amanda Keating, "Microsoft CEO Satya Nadella Shares What He's Learned About Stakeholder Capitalism as the Head of America's Most JUST Company," JUST Capital, November 5, 2020, https://justcapital.com/news/microsoft-ceo-satya-nadella-shares-leadership-lessons-on-stakeholder-capitalism/.
4. Amanda Keating, "Microsoft CEO Satya Nadella Shares What He's Learned."

5. Connie Guglielmo, "Microsoft's CEO on Helping a Faded Legend Find a 'Sense of Purpose,'" CNET, August 20, 2018, https://www.cnet.com/news/microsofts-ceo-on-helping-a-faded-legend-find-a-sense-of-purpose/.

6. Milton Friedman, "A Friedman Doctrine—The Social Responsibility of Business Is to Increase Its Profits," *New York Times*, September 13, 1970, https://www.nytimes.com/1970/09/13/archives/a-friedman-doctrine-the-social-responsibility-of-business-is-to.html.

7. George Serafeim and David Freiberg, "Harlem Capital: Changing the Face of Entrepreneurship (A)," Harvard Business School Case 120-040, October 2019, https://store.hbr.org/product/harlem-capital-changing-the-face-of-entrepreneurship-a/120040?sku=120040-PDF-ENG.

8. Paul Polman, "Full Speech: Paul Polman at the SDG Business Forum 2019," October 7, 2019, https://www.youtube.com/watch?v=JJEmG5q3m4A (video).

9. Paul Polman, "Full Speech: Paul Polman at the SDG Business Forum 2019."

10. Unilever Annual Report, https://www.unilever.com/planet-and-society/sustainability-reporting-centre/.

11. Unilever website, "About Our Strategy," https://www.unilever.co.uk/planet-and-society/our-strategy/about-our-strategy/#:~:text=Goal%3A%20By%202020%20we%20will%20enhance%20the%20livelihoods%20of%20millions,as%20we%20grow%20our%20business.&text=We%20have%20long%20known%20that,have%20evidence%20to%20prove%20this.

12. "Unilever's Purpose-Led Brands Outperform," Unilever, November 6, 2019, https://www.unilever.com/news/press-releases/2019/unilevers-purpose-led-brands-outperform.html.

13. "Unilever's Purpose-Led Brands Outperform."

14. "Business Roundtable Redefines the Purpose of a Corporation to Promote 'An Economy That Serves All Americans,'" Business Roundtable, August 19, 2019, https://www.businessroundtable.org/business-roundtable-redefines-the-purpose-of-a-corporation-to-promote-an-economy-that-serves-all-americans.

15. David Savenije, "NRG CEO; Who's Going to Empower the American Energy Consumer?" March 27, 2014, Utility Dive, https://eastcountytoday.net/antioch-police-still-looking-for-missing-man/.

16. Julia Pyper, "A Conversation with David Crane on Getting Fired from NRG and What's Next for His Energy Plans," GTM, April 29, 2014, https://www.greentechmedia.com/articles/read/a-conversation-with-david-crane.

17. NRG Energy, Progress: 2020 Sustainability Report, NRG Energy website, https://www.nrg.com/sustainability/progress.html.

18. Steve Jobs, "'You've got to find what you love,' Jobs says," Stanford University Commencement Address, June 12, 2005, https://news.stanford.edu/2005/06/14/jobs-061505/.

Chapter Two: The Impact of the "Impact Generation"

1. "Trend in Product Varieties (Number of Models) for Some Products in the USA," 2021, Springer Link website, https://link.springer.com/article/10.1057/dddmp.2013.34/tables/1.
2. "Different by Design," Aspiration website, https://www.aspiration.com/who-we-are/.
3. "Impact Report," Seventh Generation website, https://www.seventhgeneration.com/values/impact-reports.
4. "Impact Report 2019," Tesla website, https://www.tesla.com/ns_videos/2019-tesla-impact-report.pdf.
5. "Sustainability Report 2018," Oatly website, https://www.oatly.com/uploads/attachments/cjzusfwz60efmatqr5w4b6lgd-oatly-sustainability-report-web-2018-eng.pdf.
6. Richard Feloni, "PepsiCo CEO Indra Nooyi's Long-Term Strategy Put Her Job in Jeopardy—But Now the Numbers Are in, and the Analysts Who Doubted Her Will Have to Eat Their Words," *Business Insider*, February 1, 2018, https://www.businessinsider.com/indra-nooyi-pepsico-push-for-long-term-value-2018-1.
7. Julie Creswell, "Indra Nooyi, PepsiCo C.E.O. Who Pushed for Healthier Products, to Step Down," *New York Times*, August 6, 2018, https://www.nytimes.com/2018/08/06/business/indra-nooyi-pepsi.html.
8. Jens Hainmueller and Michael J. Hiscox, "Buying Green? Field Experimental Test of Consumer Support for Environmentalism," Harvard University, December 2015, https://scholar.harvard.edu/files/hiscox/files/buying_green.pdf.
9. "Edelman Trust Barometer 2021," Edelman website, https://www.edelman.com/trust/2021-trust-barometer.
10. Virginia Commonwealth University, Department of Social Welfare, https://socialwelfare.library.vcu.edu/programs/housing/company-towns-1890s-to-1935/.
11. "Survey: More Workers Find Work-Life Balance by Embracing Work-Life 'Blending,'" Enterprise Holdings, February 6, 2020, https://www.enterpriseholdings.com/en/press-archive/2020/02/surveymore-workers-find-work-life-balance-by-embracing-work-life-blending.html.

12. Joe Marino, "Must-Know Job Website Statistics (And How to Leverage Them)," Hueman, https://www.huemanrpo.com/blog/must-know-job-website-statistics.

13. Joe Marino, "Must-Know Job Website Statistics."

14. Atanas Shorgov, "How LinkedIn Learning Reached 17 Million Users in 4 Years," BetterMarketing, March 14, 2020, https://bettermarketing.pub/how-linkedin-learning-reached-17-million-users-in-4-years-59657ac55721.

15. Lauren Stewart, "How Coding Bootcamps Can Change the Face of Tech," Course Report, July 29, 2021, https://www.coursereport.com/blog/diversity-in-coding-bootcamps-report-2021.

16. "About B Corps," B Lab, https://bcorporation.net/about-b-corps#:~:text=Certified%20B%20Corporations%20are%20businesses,to%20balance%20profit%20and%20purpose.&text=B%20Corps%20form%20a%20community,as%20a%20force%20for%20good.

17. "About B Corps."

18. Michael Thomas, "Why Kickstarter Decided to Radically Transform Its Business Model," *Fast Company*, April, 12, 2017, https://www.fastcompany.com/3068547/why-kickstarter-decided-to-radically-transform-its-business-model.

19. Michael Thomas, "Why Kickstarter Decided to Radically Transform Its Business Model."

20. "Citizen Verizon," Verizon, https://www.verizon.com/about/responsibility.

21. Justine Calma, "Amazon Employees Who Spoke Out About Climate Change Could Be Fired," The Verge, January 3, 2020, https://www.theverge.com/2020/1/3/21048047/amazon-employees-climate-change-communications-policy-job-risk.

22. Johana Bhuiyan, "How the Google Walkout Transformed Tech Workers into Activists," *Los Angeles Times*, November 6, 2019, https://www.latimes.com/business/technology/story/2019-11-06/google-employee-walkout-tech-industry-activism.

23. John Paul Rollert, "The Wayfair Walkout and the Rise of Activist Capitalism," *Fortune*, July 13, 2019, https://fortune.com/2019/07/13/wayfair-nike-employee-activism/.

24. Transcript, Merck & Co., Inc. at CECP CEO Investor Forum, February 26, 2020, Thomson Reuters Streetevents, https://s21.q4cdn.com/488056881/files/doc_downloads/transcripts/MRK-USQ_Transcript_2018-02-26.pdf.

25. Transcript, Merck & Co Inc at CECP CEO Investor Forum.

26. Leslie Gaines-Ross, "4 in 10 American Workers Consider Themselves Social Activists," Quartz, September 20, 2019, https://qz.com/work/1712492/how-employee-activists-are-changing-the-workplace/.

27. Johana Bhuiyan, "How the Google Walkout Transformed Tech Workers into Activists."

28. Paige Leskin, "Uber Says the #DeleteUber Movement Led to 'Hundreds of Thousands' of People Quitting the App," *Business Insider*, April 11, 2019, https://www.businessinsider.com/uber-deleteuber-protest-hundreds -of-thousands-quit-app-2019-4.

29. Stephie Grob Plante, "Shopping Has Become a Politiccal Act. Here's How It Happened," Vox, October 7, 2019, https://www.vox.com/the -goods/2019/10/7/20894134/consumer-activism-conscious-consumerism -explained.

30. Sarah Title, "What Ecommerce Brands Need to Know About Consumer Activism by Generation," Digital Commerce 360, July 27, 2020, https:// www.digitalcommerce360.com/2020/07/27/what-ecommerce-brands -need-to-know-about-consumer-activism-by-generation/.

31. Stephie Grob Plante, "Shopping Has Become a Political Act. Here's How It Happened."

32. Kathy Gurchiek, "Employee Activism Is on the Rise," SHRM (Society for Human Resource Management), September 12, 2019, https://www.shrm .org/hr-today/news/hr-news/pages/employee-activism-on-the-rise.aspx.

33. Carol Cone, "10 Ways Purposeful Business Will Evolve in 2020," *Fast Company*, January 13, 2020, https://www.fastcompany.com/90450734/10-ways -purposeful-business-will-evolve-in-2020.

34. Claudine Gartenberg, Andrea Prat, and George Serafeim, "Corporate Purpose and Financial Performance," *Organization Science* 30, no. 1 (January–February 2019), pp. 1–18.

35. Claudine Gartenberg, Andrea Prat, and George Serafeim, "Corporate Purpose and Financial Performance."

36. Claudine Gartenberg and George Serafeim, "Corporate Purpose in Public and Private Firms," Harvard Business School Working Paper, No. 20-024, August 2019 (Revised July 2020), https://papers.ssrn.com/sol3/papers .cfm?abstract_id=3440281.

37. Tom Foster, "Do You Really Want Your Business to Go Public?" *Inc.*, October 2015, https://www.inc.com/thomson-reuters/workforce-management-in -the-covid-19-era.html.

38. Claudine Gartenberg and George Serafeim, "Corporate Purpose in Public and Private Firms."

39. Vanessa C. Burbano, "Social Responsibility Messages and Worker Wage Requirements: Field Experimental Evidence from Online Labor Marketplaces," *Organization Science* 27, no. 4 (June 30, 2016), https://pubsonline .informs.org/doi/abs/10.1287/orsc.2016.1066; Vanessa C. Burbano,

"Getting Gig Workers to Do More by Doing Good: Field Experimental Evidence from Online Platform Labor Marketplaces," *Organization & Environment* (June 24, 2019), https://papers.ssrn.com/sol3/papers.cfm?abstract_id=3405689.

Chapter Three: Transparency and Accountability: No More Secrets

1. Robert G. Eccles and George Serafeim, "Foxconn Technology Group (A) and (B) (TN)," Harvard Business School Teaching Note 413-055, August 2012 (Revised March 2013).

2. M. R. Wong, W. McKelvey, K. Ito, C. Schiff, J. B. Jacobson, and D. Kass, "Impact of a Letter-Grade Program on Restaurant Sanitary Conditions and Diner Behavior in New York City," *American Journal of Public Health* 105, no. 3 (2015), e81–e87. doi:10.2105/AJPH.2014.302404.

3. Melanie J. Firestone and Craig W. Hedberg, "Restaurant Inspection Letter Grades and Salmonella Infections, New York, New York, USA," *Emerging Infectious Diseases Journal* 24, no. 12 (December 2018), https://wwwnc.cdc.gov/eid/article/24/12/18-0544_article.

4. *TSC Indus. v. Northway, Inc.*, 426 U.S. 438, 449 (1976).

5. Robert G. Eccles and George Serafeim, "Sustainability in Financial Services Is Not About Being Green," *Harvard Business Review*, May 15, 2013, https://hbr.org/2013/05/sustainability-in-financial-services-is-not-about-being-green.

6. Jody Grewal, Clarissa Hauptmann, and George Serafeim, "Material Sustainability Information and Stock Price Informativeness," *Journal of Business Ethics* 171, no. 3 (July 2021), pp. 513–544, https://papers.ssrn.com/sol3/papers.cfm?abstract_id=2966144.

7. Lucy Handley and Sam Meredith, "Danone Hopes It's Blazing a Trail by Adopting a New Earnings Metric to Expose the Cost of Carbon Emission," CNBC, October 21, 2020, https://www.cnbc.com/2020/10/21/danone-adopts-earnings-metric-to-expose-the-cost-of-carbon-emissions.html.

8. Lucy Handley and Sam Meredith, "Danone Hopes It's Blazing a Trail by Adopting a New Earnings Metric."

Chapter Four: The Evolving Consequences of Corporate Behavior

1. Drew Desilver, "As Coronavirus Spreads, Which U.S. Workers Have Paid Sick Leave—And Which Don't?" Pew Research Center, March 12, 2020, https://www.pewresearch.org/fact-tank/2020/03/12/as-coronavirus-spreads-which-u-s-workers-have-paid-sick-leave-and-which-dont/.

2. Richard Carufel, "Edelman's New Trust Barometer Finds CEOs Failing to Meet Today's Leadership Expectations," Agility PR Solutions, May 2, 2019, https://www.agilitypr.com/pr-news/public-relations/edelmans-new-trust-barometer-finds-ceos-failing-to-meet-todays-leadership-expectations/.

3. "Trust in Government: 1958–2015," Pew Research Center, November 23, 2015, https://www.pewresearch.org/politics/2015/11/23/1-trust-in-government-1958-2015; "Americans' Views of Government: Low Trust, but Some Positive Performance Ratings," Pew Research Center, September 14, 2020, https://www.pewresearch.org/politics/2020/09/14/americans-views-of-government-low-trust-but-some-positive-performance-ratings/.

4. "With No Time to Lose, Grupo Bimbo Takes the Lead on Sustainability," Baking Business, October, 14, 2019, https://www.bakingbusiness.com/articles/49587-with-no-time-to-lose-grupo-bimbo-takes-the-lead-on-sustainability.

5. Adrian Gore, "How Discovery Keeps Innovating," McKinsey & Company, June 2015, https://healthcare.mckinsey.com/how-discovery-keeps-innovating/.

6. Simon Mainwaring, "Why Purpose Is Paramount to Business and Branding Success: A Walmart Case Study," *Forbes*, August 18, 2017, https://www.forbes.com/sites/simonmainwaring/2017/08/18/why-purpose-is-paramount-to-business-and-branding-success-a-walmart-case-study/?sh=2cc3b73f69bb.

7. "Our Commitments," Natura website, https://www.naturabrasil.com/pages/our-commitments.

8. Anita M. McGahan and Leandro S. Pongeluppe, "There Is No Planet B: Stakeholder Governance That Aligns Incentives to Preserve the Amazon Rainforest," January 21, 2020, https://www.hbs.edu/faculty/Shared%20Documents/conferences/strategy-science-2021/30_Leandro%20Pongeluppe_There%20Is%20No%20Planet%20B%20Stakeholder%20Governance%20That%20Aligns%20Incentives%20To%20Preserve%20The%20Amazon%20Rainforest.pdf.

9. JUST Report, "The COVID-19 Corporate Response Tracker: How America's Largest Employers Are Treating Stakeholders Amid the Coronavirus Crisis," JUST Capital, https://justcapital.com/reports/the-covid-19-corporate-response-tracker-how-americas-largest-employers-are-treating-stakeholders-amid-the-coronavirus-crisis/.

10. JUST Report, "The COVID-19 Corporate Response Tracker: How America's Largest Employers Are Treating Stakeholders Amid the Coronavirus Crisis."

11. Richard Kestenbaum, "LVMH Converting Its Perfume Factories to Make Hand Sanitizer," *Forbes*, March 15, 2020, https://www.forbes.com/sites

/richardkestenbaum/2020/03/15/lvmh-converting-its-perfume-factories
-to-make-hand-sanitizer/?sh=fe2fc704a9a0#:~:text=LVMH%20announced
%20today%20that%20it,to%20make%20hand%20sanitizer%20instead
.&text=It%20is%20also%20justifying%20having,its%20employees%20
coming%20to%20work.

12. "Zoom for Education," Zoom, https://zoom.us/education.

13. Alex Cheema-Fox, Bridget LaPerla, George Serafeim, and Hui (Stacie) Wang, "Corporate Resilience and Response During COVID-19," Harvard Business School Accounting & Management Unit Working Paper No. 20-108 (September 23, 2020), http://dx.doi.org/10.2139/ssrn.3578167.

14. Letitia James, "Attorney General James Sues New York Sports Club and Lucille Roberts for Charging Illegal Dues and Prohibiting Consumers from Canceling Memberships," press release, September 30, 2020, https://ag.ny .gov/press-release/2020/attorney-general-james-sues-new-york-sports-club -and-lucille-roberts-charging.

15. Tonya Riley, "WeWork Under Pressure as More Members Contract Coronavirus in Co-working Spaces," *Washington Post*, March 20, 2020, https://www .washingtonpost.com/technology/2020/03/20/wework-under-pressure -more-members-contract-coronavirus-co-working-spaces/.

16. Zack Beauchamp, "Brazil's Petrobras Scandal, Explained," Vox, March 18, 2016, https://www.vox.com/2016/3/18/11260924/petrobras-brazil.

17. David Segal, "Petrobras Oil Scandal Leaves Brazilians Lamenting a Lost Dream," *New York Times*, August 7, 2015, https://www.nytimes.com/2015/08 /09/business/international/effects-of-petrobras-scandal-leave-brazilians -lamenting-a-lost-dream.html.

18. "Former Petrobras CEO Sentenced to 11 Years in Jail," AP, March 7, 2018, https://www.nytimes.com/2015/08/09/business/international/effects -of-petrobras-scandal-leave-brazilians-lamenting-a-lost-dream.html.

19. Siri Schubert and T. Christian Miller, "At Siemens, Bribery Was Just a Line Item," *New York Times*, December 20, 2008, https://www.nytimes .com/2008/12/21/business/worldbusiness/21siemens.html.

20. Sudip Kar-Gupta and Tim Hepher, "Airbus Faces Record $4 Billion Fine After Bribery Probe," January 27, 2020, Reuters, https://www .reuters.com/article/us-airbus-probe/airbus-faces-record-4-billion-fine -after-bribery-probe-idUSKBN1ZR0HQ.

21. Boris Groysberg, Eric Lin, and George Serafeim, "Does Corporate Misconduct Affect the Future Compensation of Alumni Managers?" Special Issue on Employee Inter- and Intra-Firm Mobility, *Advances in Strategic Management* 41 (July 2020), https://www.emerald.com/insight/content/doi/10.1108 /S0742-332220200000041020/full/html.

Chapter Five: The Tactical Path to Profitably Doing Good

1. David Freiberg, Jody Grewal, and George Serafeim, "Science-Based Carbon Emissions Targets," Harvard Business School Working Paper, No. 21-108, March 2021, https://papers.ssrn.com/sol3/papers.cfm?abstract_id=3804530.
2. "About Us," Vital Farms website, https://vitalfarms.com/about-us/.
3. Interview with Ori Zohar.
4. Interview with Ori Zohar.

Chapter Six: The Archetypes of Opportunity: How Companies Capture Value

1. Simon Mainwaring, "Purpose at Work: Warby Parker's Keys to Success," *Forbes*, December 1, 2020, https://www.forbes.com/sites/simonmainwaring/2020/12/01/purpose-at-work-warby-parkers-keys-to-success/?sh=3a6fc675dba7.
2. "2021 Global 100 Ranking," Corporate Knights, January 25, 2021, https://www.corporateknights.com/reports/2021-global-100/2021-global-100-ranking-16115328/.
3. "Ørsted's Renewable-Energy Transformation," Interview, McKinsey & Company, July 10, 2020.
4. "Ørsted's Renewable-Energy Transformation," Interview.
5. "Ørsted's Renewable-Energy Transformation," Interview.
6. "Aluminum Cans—History, Development, and Market," AZO Materials, June 24, 2002, https://www.azom.com/article.aspx?ArticleID=1483.
7. Laura Parker, "The World's Plastic Pollution Crisis Explained," *National Geographic*, June 7, 2019, https://www.nationalgeographic.com/environment/article/plastic-pollution.
8. "The Toxic 100: Top Corporate Air Polluters in the United States, 2010," Infoplease, https://www.infoplease.com/math-science/earth-environment/the-toxic-100-top-corporate-air-polluters-in-the-united-states-2010.
9. "2020 Sustainability Report," Ball Corporation, https://www.ball.com/getmedia/b25d3346-b8ca-4e3f-9cce-562101dd8cd7/Ball-SR20-Web_FINAL.pdf.aspx.
10. Angelo Young, "Coca-Cola, Pepsi Highlight the 20 Corporations Producing the Most Ocean Pollution," *USA Today*, June 17, 2019, https://www.usatoday.com/story/money/2019/06/17/20-corporations-behind-the-most-ocean-pollution/39552009/.
11. "Clean Energy Group NextEra Surpasses ExxonMobil in Market Cap," *Financial Times*, October 2, 2020, https://www.ft.com/content/39a70458-d4d1-4a6e-aca6-1d5670bade11.

12. "Clean Growth," AES website, https://www.aes.com/sustainability/clean-growth-and-innovation.

Chapter Seven: Investors Driving Change: More Than Negative Screening

1. "Frequently Asked Questions," Reenergize Exxon, https://reenergizexom.com/faqs/.
2. Shelley Vinyard, "Investors' Directive to P&G: Stop Driving Deforestation," NRDC, October 14, 2020, https://www.nrdc.org/experts/shelley-vinyard/investors-directive-pg-stop-driving-deforestation.
3. Climate Action 100+ website, https://www.climateaction100.org.
4. Rebecca Chapman and Gerald Nabor, "How Investors Can Support Circular Economy for Plastics: New Engagement Guidance," Principles for Responsible Investment, https://www.unpri.org.
5. Ioannis Ioannou and George Serafeim, "The Impact of Corporate Social Responsibility on Investment Recommendations: Analysts' Perceptions and Shifting Institutional Logics," *Strategic Management Journal* 36, no. 7 (July 2015), pp. 1053–1081, https://papers.ssrn.com/sol3/papers.cfm?abstract_id=1507874.
6. George Serafeim, "Public Sentiment and the Price of Corporate Sustainability," *Financial Analysts Journal* 76, no. 2 (2020), pp. 26–46, https://papers.ssrn.com/sol3/papers.cfm?abstract_id=3265502.
7. "Tailored Strategies," The Carlyle Group, 2018, https://www.carlyle.com/sites/default/files/reports/carlyleccr2018_0.pdf.
8. "Risks, Opportunities, and Investment in the Era of Climate Change," Harvard Business School, March 4, 2020, https://www.alumni.hbs.edu/events/invest20/Pages/default.aspx.
9. "Novartis Reinforces Commitment to Patient Access, Pricing a EUR 1.85 Billion Sustainability-Linked Bond," Novartis, September 16, 2020, https://www.novartis.com/news/media-releases/novartis-reinforces-commitment-patient-access-pricing-eur-185-billion-sustainability-linked-bond.
10. Mike Turner, "SLB Champion Enel Plans First Sterling Trade Using Structure," Global Capital, October 12, 2020, https://www.globalcapital.com/article/b1ns66gtysc8d4/slb-champion-enel-plans-first-sterling-trade-using-structure.
11. Decarbonization Advisory Panel, "Beliefs and Recommendations," April 2019, https://www.osc.state.ny.us/files/reports/special-topics/pdf/decarbonization-advisory-panel-2019.pdf.
12. Make My Money Matter website, https://makemymoneymatter.co.uk.

13. George Serafeim, "Investors as Stewards of the Commons?" *Journal of Applied Corporate Finance* 30, no. 2 (Spring 2018): 8–17, https://papers.ssrn.com/sol3/papers.cfm?abstract_id=3014952.

14. Cyrus Taraporevala, "Fearless Girl's Shattered Ceilings: Why Diversity in Leadership Matters," State Street Global Advisors, March 8, 2021, https://www.ssga.com/us/en/institutional/ic/insights/fearless-girls-shattered-ceilings-why-diversity-in-leadership.

Chapter Eight: Alignment: Now or Later?

1. Robert G. Eccles, Kathleen Miller Perkins, and George Serafeim, "How to Become a Sustainable Company," *MIT Sloan Management Review* 53, no. 4 (Summer 2012): 43–50, https://www.hbs.edu/ris/Publication%20Files/SMR_Article_EcclesMillerSerafeim_77d4247b-d715-447d-8e79-74a6ec893f40.pdf.

2. "We Were Coming Up Against Everything from Organized Crime to Angry Employees," Interview with Erik Osmundsen, *Harvard Business Review*, July–August 2019, https://hbr.org/2019/07/we-were-coming-up-against-everything-from-organized-crime-to-angry-employees.

3. "We Were Coming Up Against Everything from Organized Crime to Angry Employees," Interview with Erik Osmundsen.

4. C. I. Barnard, *The Functions of the Executive* (Cambridge, MA: Harvard University Press, 1938).

5. P. Selznick, *Leadership in Administration: A Sociological Interpretation* (Evanston, IL: Row Peterson, 1957).

Conclusion: The Future of Purpose and Profit

1. "Danone: A Case Study in the Pitfalls of Purpose," *Financial Times*, https://www.ft.com/content/668d9544-28db-4ad7-9870-1f6671623ac5.

2. Amelia Lucas, "Chipotle Will Link Executive Compensation to Environment Diversity Goals," March 4, 2021, CNBC, https://www.ft.com/content/668d9544-28db-4ad7-9870-1f6671623ac5; Kevin Orland, "CEO Pay Tied to ESG Sets Canadian Banks Apart from the Crowd," Bloomberg, March 18, 2021, https://www.bloomberg.com/news/articles/2021-03-18/ceo-pay-tied-to-esg-sets-canadian-banks-apart-from-the-crowd.

BIBLIOGRAPHY

The topics covered in this book emerge from the research that a variety of colleagues and I have conducted over the past decade-plus. For more detail on the major topics in the book, I have included citations under each chapter heading below where you can find the original papers. Where those papers are referred to in the text, I have not called them out with specific endnotes, but where I cite the work of others, or rely on any sources aside from work I have contributed to, those points are flagged in the text and listed below.

Introduction

Alex Cheema-Fox, Bridget LaPerla, George Serafeim, and Hui (Stacie) Wang. "Corporate Resilience and Response During COVID-19." *Journal of Applied Corporate Finance*. 2021.

Ioannis Ioannou and George Serafeim. "The Impact of Corporate Social Responsibility on Investment Recommendations: Analysts' Perceptions and Shifting Institutional Logics." *Strategic Management Journal* 36, no. 7 (July 2015): 1053–1081.

Mozaffar Khan, George Serafeim, and Aaron Yoon. "Corporate Sustainability: First Evidence on Materiality." *Accounting Review* 91, no. 6 (November 2016).

Chapter One: The Business of Being in Business: What Has Changed

George Serafeim and David Freiberg. "Harlem Capital: Changing the Face of Entrepreneurship (A)." Harvard Business School Case 120-040, October 2019.

George Serafeim and David Freiberg. "Harlem Capital: Changing the Face of Entrepreneurship (B)." Harvard Business School Supplement 120-041, October 2019.

George Serafeim and David Freiberg. "Summa Equity: Building Purpose-Driven Organizations." Harvard Business School Case 118-028, November 2017. (Revised April 2019.)

George Serafeim, Ethan Rouen, and Sarah Gazzaniga. "Redefining Mogul." Harvard Business School Case 120-043, March 2020. (Revised May 2020.)

Chapter Two: The Impact of the "Impact Generation"

Claudine Gartenberg, Andrea Prat, and George Serafeim. "Corporate Purpose and Financial Performance." *Organization Science* 30, no. 1 (January–February 2019): 1–18.

Claudine Gartenberg and George Serafeim. "Corporate Purpose in Public and Private Firms." Harvard Business School Working Paper, No. 20-024, August 2019. (Revised July 2020.)

George Serafeim and Claudine Gartenberg. "The Type of Purpose That Makes Companies More Profitable." *Harvard Business Review* (website) (October 21, 2016).

Chapter Three: Transparency and Accountability: No More Secrets

Dane Christensen, George Serafeim, and Anywhere Sikochi. "Why Is Corporate Virtue in the Eye of the Beholder? The Case of ESG Ratings." *Accounting Review* 97, no. 1 (January 2022): 147–175.

Ronald Cohen and George Serafeim. "How to Measure a Company's Real Impact." *Harvard Business Review* (website) (September 3, 2020).

Robert G. Eccles and George Serafeim. "Sustainability in Financial Services Is Not About Being Green." *Harvard Business Review Blogs* (May 15, 2013).

Robert G. Eccles, George Serafeim, and Beiting Cheng. "Foxconn Technology Group (A)." Harvard Business School Case 112–002, July 2011. (Revised June 2013.)

Robert G. Eccles, George Serafeim, and Beiting Cheng. "Foxconn Technology Group (B)." Harvard Business School Supplement 112-058, November 2011. (Revised February 2012.)

Jody Grewal, Clarissa Hauptmann, and George Serafeim. "Material Sustainability Information and Stock Price Informativeness." *Journal of Business Ethics* 171, no. 3 (July 2021): 513–544.

Jody Grewal and George Serafeim. "Research on Corporate Sustainability: Review and Directions for Future Research." (pdf) *Foundations and Trends® in Accounting* 14, no. 2 (2020): 73–127.

Ioannis Ioannou and George Serafeim. "The Consequences of Mandatory Corporate Sustainability Reporting." In *The Oxford Handbook of Corporate Social Responsibility: Psychological and Organizational Perspectives*, edited by Abagail McWilliams, Deborah E. Rupp, Donald S. Siegel, Günter K. Stahl, and David A. Waldman, 452–489. Oxford University Press, 2019.

Sakis Kotsantonis and George Serafeim. "Four Things No One Will Tell You About ESG Data." *Journal of Applied Corporate Finance* 31, no. 2 (Spring 2019): 50–58.

Ethan Rouen and George Serafeim. "Impact-Weighted Financial Accounts: A Paradigm Shift." *CESifo Forum* 22, no. 3 (May 2021): 20–25.

George Serafeim, Vincent Dessain, and Mette Fuglsang Hjortshoej. "Sustainable Product Management at Solvay." Harvard Business School Case 120-081, February 2020.

George Serafeim and Jody Grewal. "ESG Metrics: Reshaping Capitalism?" Harvard Business School Technical Note 116-037, March 2016. (Revised April 2019.)

George Serafeim and Katie Trinh. "A Framework for Product Impact-Weighted Accounts." Harvard Business School Working Paper, No. 20-076, January 2020.

George Serafeim, T. Robert Zochowski, and Jennifer Downing. "Impact-Weighted Financial Accounts: The Missing Piece for an Impact Economy." (pdf) White Paper, Harvard Business School, Boston, September 2019.

Chapter Four: The Evolving Consequences of Corporate Behavior

Alex Cheema-Fox, Bridget LaPerla, George Serafeim, and Hui (Stacie) Wang. "Corporate Resilience and Response During COVID-19." *Journal of Applied Corporate Finance*. 2021.

Robert G. Eccles, George Serafeim, and James Heffernan. "Natura Cosméticos, S.A." Harvard Business School Case 412-052, November 2011. (Revised June 2013.)

Claudine Gartenberg and George Serafeim. "181 Top CEOs Have Realized Companies Need a Purpose Beyond Profit." *Harvard Business Review* (website) (August 20, 2019).

Boris Groysberg, Eric Lin, and George Serafeim. "Does Corporate Misconduct Affect the Future Compensation of Alumni Managers?" Special Issue on Employee Inter- and Intra-Firm Mobility. *Advances in Strategic Management* 41 (July 2020).

Boris Groysberg, Eric Lin, George Serafeim, and Robin Abrahams. "The Scandal Effect." *Harvard Business Review* 94, no. 9 (September 2016): 90–98.

Paul M. Healy and George Serafeim. "An Analysis of Firms' Self-Reported Anticorruption Efforts." *Accounting Review* 91, no. 2 (March 2016): 489–511.

Paul M. Healy and George Serafeim. "How to Scandal-Proof Your Company." *Harvard Business Review* 97, no. 4 (July–August 2019): 42–50.

Paul M. Healy and George Serafeim. "Who Pays for White-Collar Crime?" Harvard Business School Working Paper, No. 16-148, June 2016.

George Serafeim, "Facebook, BlackRock, and the Case for Purpose-Driven Companies." *Harvard Business Review* (website) (January 16, 2018).

George Serafeim, "The Role of the Corporation in Society: An Alternative View and Opportunities for Future Research." Harvard Business School Working Paper, No. 14-110, May 2014.

Chapter Five: The Tactical Path to Profitably Doing Good

Francois Brochet, Maria Loumioti, and George Serafeim. "Speaking of the Short-Term: Disclosure Horizon and Managerial Myopia." *Review of Accounting Studies* 20, no. 3 (September 2015): 1122–1163.

Beiting Cheng, Ioannis Ioannou, and George Serafeim. "Corporate Social Responsibility and Access to Finance." *Strategic Management Journal* 35, no. 1 (January 2014): 1–23.

Robert G. Eccles, Ioannis Ioannou, and George Serafeim. "The Impact of Corporate Sustainability on Organizational Processes and Performance." (pdf) *Management Science* 60, no. 11 (November 2014): 2835–2857.

Ioannis Ioannou, Shelley Xin Li, and George Serafeim. "The Effect of Target Difficulty on Target Completion: The Case of Reducing Carbon Emissions." *Accounting Review* 91, no. 5 (September 2016).

Robert G. Eccles, George Serafeim, and Shelley Xin Li. "Dow Chemical: Innovating for Sustainability." Harvard Business School Case 112-064, January 2012. (Revised June 2013.)

David Freiberg, Jody Grewal, and George Serafeim. "Science-Based Carbon Emissions Targets." Harvard Business School Working Paper, No. 21-108, March 2021.

David Freiberg, Jean Rogers, and George Serafeim. "How ESG Issues Become Financially Material to Corporations and Their Investors." Harvard Business School Working Paper, No. 20-056, November 2019. (Revised November 2020.)

Jody Grewal and George Serafeim. "Research on Corporate Sustainability: Review and Directions for Future Research." (pdf) *Foundations and Trends® in Accounting* 14, no. 2 (2020): 73–127.

Ioannis Ioannou and George Serafeim. "Corporate Sustainability: A Strategy?" Harvard Business School Working Paper, No. 19-065, January 2019. (Revised April 2021.)

Ioannis Ioannou and George Serafeim. "Yes, Sustainability Can Be a Strategy." *Harvard Business Review* (website) (February 11, 2019).

Kathy Miller and George Serafeim. "Chief Sustainability Officers: Who Are They and What Do They Do?" Chap. 8 in *Leading Sustainable Change: An Organizational Perspective*, edited by Rebecca Henderson, Ranjay Gulati, and Michael Tushman. Oxford University Press, 2015.

George Serafeim and David Freiberg. "JetBlue: Relevant Sustainability Leadership (A)." Harvard Business School Case 118-030, October 2017. (Revised October 2018.)

George Serafeim and David Freiberg. "JetBlue: Relevant Sustainability Leadership (B)." Harvard Business School Supplement 119-044, October 2018.

George Serafeim and David Freiberg. "Turnaround at Norsk Gjenvinning (B)." Harvard Business School Supplement 118-033, October 2017.

George Serafeim and Shannon Gombos. "Turnaround at Norsk Gjenvinning (A)." Harvard Business School Case 116-012, August 2015. (Revised October 2017.)

George Serafeim and Aaron Yoon. "Stock Price Reactions to ESG News: The Role of ESG Ratings and Disagreement." *Review of Accounting Studies*, forthcoming (2022).

George Serafeim and Aaron Yoon. "Which Corporate ESG News Does the Market React To?" *Financial Analysts Journal* 78, no. 1 (2022): 59–78.

Chapter Six: The Archetypes of Opportunity: How Companies Capture Value

Robert G. Eccles, George Serafeim, and Shelley Xin Li. "Dow Chemical: Innovating for Sustainability." Harvard Business School Case 112-064, January 2012. (Revised June 2013.)

George Serafeim. "Social-Impact Efforts That Create Real Value." *Harvard Business Review* 98, no. 5 (September–October 2020): 38–48.

George Serafeim. "The Type of Socially Responsible Investments That Make Firms More Profitable." *Harvard Business Review* (website) (April 14, 2015).

Chapter Seven: Investors Driving Change: More Than Negative Screening

Amir Amel-Zadeh and George Serafeim. "Why and How Investors Use ESG Information: Evidence from a Global Survey." *Financial Analysts Journal* 74, no. 3 (Third Quarter 2018): 87–103.

Rohit Deshpandé, Aiyesha Dey, and George Serafeim. "BlackRock: Linking Purpose to Profit." Harvard Business School Case 120-042, January 2020. (Revised July 2020.)

Rebecca Henderson, George Serafeim, Josh Lerner, and Naoko Jinjo. "Should a Pension Fund Try to Change the World? Inside GPIF's Embrace of ESG." Harvard Business School Case 319-067, January 2019. (Revised February 2020).

Ioannis Ioannou and George Serafeim. "The Impact of Corporate Social Responsibility on Investment Recommendations: Analysts' Perceptions and Shifting Institutional Logics." *Strategic Management Journal* 36, no. 7 (July 2015): 1053–1081.

Mindy Lubber and George Serafeim. "3 Ways Investors Can Pressure Companies to Take Sustainability Seriously." *Barron's* (June 23, 2019).

Michael E. Porter, George Serafeim, and Mark Kramer. "Where ESG Fails." *Institutional Investor* (October 16, 2019).

Christina Rehnberg, George Serafeim, and Brian Tomlinson. "Why CEOs Should Share Their Long-Term Plans with Investors." *Harvard Business Review* (website) (September 19, 2018).

George Serafeim. "Can Index Funds Be a Force for Sustainable Capitalism?" *Harvard Business Review* (website) (December 7, 2017).

George Serafeim. "ESG Returns Eventually Will Win Over Critics." *Barron's* (March 1, 2019).

George Serafeim. "How Index Funds Can Be a Positive Force for Change." *Barron's* (October 12, 2018).

George Serafeim. "Investors as Stewards of the Commons?" *Journal of Applied Corporate Finance* 30, no. 2 (Spring 2018): 8–17.

George Serafeim. "Public Sentiment and the Price of Corporate Sustainability." *Financial Analysts Journal* 76, no. 2 (2020): 26–46.

George Serafeim. "The Fastest-Growing Cause for Shareholders Is Sustainability." *Harvard Business Review* (website) (July 12, 2016).

George Serafeim and David Freiberg. "Summa Equity: Building Purpose-Driven Organizations." Harvard Business School Case 118-028, November 2017. (Revised April 2019.)

George Serafeim and Mark Fulton. "Divestment Alone Won't Beat Climate Change." *Harvard Business Review* (website) (November 4, 2014).

George Serafeim and Sakis Kotsantonis. "ExxonMobil's Shareholder Vote Is a Tipping Point for Climate Issues." *Harvard Business Review* (website) (June 7, 2017).

George Serafeim, Shiva Rajgopal, and David Freiberg. "ExxonMobil: Business as Usual? (A)." Harvard Business School Case 117-046, February 2017. (Revised June 2017.)

George Serafeim, Shiva Rajgopal, and David Freiberg. "ExxonMobil: Business as Usual? (B)." Harvard Business School Supplement 117-047, February 2017. (Revised June 2017.)

Chapter Eight: Alignment: Now or Later?

George Serafeim. "4 Ways Managers Can Exercise Their 'Agency' to Change the World." https://hbswk.hbs.edu/item/4-ways-managers-can-exercise-their-agency-to-change-the-world.

George Serafeim and David Freiberg. "Turnaround at Norsk Gjenvinning (B)." Harvard Business School Supplement 118-033, October 2017.

George Serafeim and Shannon Gombos. "Turnaround at Norsk Gjenvinning (A)." Harvard Business School Case 116-012, August 2015. (Revised October 2017.)

Conclusion: The Future of Purpose and Profit

Ethan Rouen and George Serafeim. "Impact-Weighted Financial Accounts: A Paradigm Shift." CESifo Forum 22, no. 3 (May 2021): 20–25.

INDEX

ABOUT THE AUTHOR

GEORGE SERAFEIM is the Charles M. Williams Professor of Business Administration at Harvard Business School. One of the youngest faculty members to receive tenure at Harvard Business School, he has presented his research in more than sixty countries around the world, including to world leaders in government and business at events such as the World Economic Forum at Davos, the Aspen Ideas Festival, White House conferences on business leadership, the Securities and Exchange Commission, and the European Commission. He ranks among the top-ten most popular authors out of more than twelve thousand business authors on the Social Science Research Network.

George has received multiple awards and recognitions, including the Pericles Leadership Award in recognition of his service to the Hellenic Republic and numerous awards for his research on corporate purpose, sustainability, and the integration of environmental, social, and governance (ESG) issues into business strategy and investing, including the Kim B. Clark Fellowship on Responsible Leadership at Oxford University, the Dr. Richard A. Crowell Memorial Prize, and the Graham and Dodd Scroll Award. A recognized leader, he cofounded the leading sustainability strategy consulting firm KKS Advisors and is an academic partner at State Street Associates, a unit of one of the largest custodian banks in the world. He serves on the board of directors of both Liberty Mutual, a Fortune 100 company and global leader in property-casualty insurance, and dss+, a leading operations consulting firm and the global leader in employee health and safety services.

Prior to that, he served on the steering committee of the Athens Exchange Group, the governance body for both stock and bond market exchanges, with a focus on capital formation and efficient financing, and as the chairperson of Greece's Corporate Governance Council. During his tenure, a new corporate governance code was created and issued to improve corporate governance practices, investor protection, and competitiveness.

He has also contributed to advancing corporate transparency globally, having served on the inaugural Standards Council of the Sustainability Accounting Standards Board, which created standards for investor-relevant sustainability corporate disclosures adopted by hundreds of leading companies around the world, and on the Taskforce Working Group on Impact Transparency, Integrity, and Reporting established by the UK's G7 Presidency.